Pray, Love, Remember

Pray, Love, Remember

MICHAEL MAYNE

Foreword by
ALAN BENNETT

DARTON · LONGMAN + TODD

First published in 1998 by
Darton, Longman and Todd Ltd
1 Spencer Court
140–142 Wandsworth High Street
London SW18 4JJ

Reprinted 1999, 2000 and 2005

ISBN 0–232–52270–7

A catalogue record for this book is available from the British
Library.

Thanks are due to the following for permission to use copyright
material: Beacon Press, Boston for 'When Death Comes' taken
from *New and Selected Poems* by Mary Oliver © 1992; Carcanet
Press for 'Flying Crooked' by Robert Graves; W. W. Norton and
Company for 'i am a little church (no great cathedral)' taken from
Complete Poems 1904–1962 by E. E. Cummings, edited by George
J. Firmage, © 1991 by the Trustees for the E. E. Cummings Trust
and George J. Firmage; Macmillan General Books for 'Folk Tale',
'Waiting' and 'The Word' by R. S. Thomas; Mowbray, an imprint
of Cassell PLC, for 'God is Love' by Timothy Rees.

Designed by Sandie Boccacci
Set in 9/12.25 pt Stone Serif by Intype London Ltd
Printed and bound in Great Britain by
Page Bros, Norwich Norfolk

For all with whom I worked at the Abbey
1986–96
whose dedication and loyalty made it
an incomparably rich and diverse community

With my affection and gratitude

There's rosemary, that's for remembrance; pray,
love, remember.

Hamlet IV, 5

To discover how to be human now
Is the reason we follow this star.

W. H. Auden, *For the Time Being*

What is the meaning of life? That was all – a
simple question; one that tended to close in on
one with the years. The great revelation had
never come. The great revelation perhaps never
did come. Instead there were little daily miracles,
illuminations, matches struck unexpectedly in
the dark.

Virginia Woolf, *To the Lighthouse*

Contents

Foreword by Alan Bennett   xi
Introduction   xv

Chapter 1   ASH WEDNESDAY   1
            The Tomb of the Unknown Warrior
            On being human

Chapter 2   LENT I   15
            St Faith's Chapel
            On being tempted; and on prayer

Chapter 3   LENT II   29
            The Nave and Quire
            On valid and invalid expectations; on role-playing
            and integrity

Chapter 4   LENT III   47
            St Edward's Shrine
            On suffering, loneliness and vulnerability

Chapter 5   MID-LENT BREATHER   61
            Poets' Corner
            On words and the Word

Chapter 6   LENT IV   75
            The West Front
            On self-giving love; and on our proper end

CONTENTS

Chapter 7   LENT V   90
             The Innocent Victims' Memorial
             On remembering the innocent

Chapter 8   PALM SUNDAY   101
             The Abbot's Pew
             On our public and private selves; on human rights
             and on dying well

Chapter 9   EASTER DAY   119
             The Abbey
             On the hope of resurrection; and on being
             re-membered

Notes   136

Foreword

To understand why I am writing this foreword one has to go back to an evening in January 1991. The Dean of Westminster, Michael Mayne, whom I have never met, has asked me if I would do a poetry reading, one of a series he puts on at the Abbey in support of AIDS charities. It is the day of the West's entry into the Gulf War and as I drive to the Abbey I listen on the car radio to the debate in the Commons, noting the unanimity of opinion, usually described as 'the House of Commons at its best' but which often signifies the opposite: as I listen only Clare Short raises a doubting voice. The reading is in the Jerusalem Chamber with one or two of the poems – Hardy's 'Gunner Hodge', for instance, and Larkin's 'MCMXIV' – tonight acquiring an awful poignancy in the light of events in the desert.

Afterwards Michael takes me round the darkened Abbey where, other than for memorial services, I have never been. We stand on the steps of the High Altar looking down the nave and although I heartily disapprove of this war and its motives I feel glad to be at this time in this place which has seen wars come and go and bears their memorials and which houses in the Unknown Warrior the most famous and yet least known of all those who have fallen in battle.

Then we go up the back way through the Abbot's Pew and Jericho Parlour into the Deanery where Alison has made a delicious supper which we have round the Aga while watching the Prime Minister's statement on television.

Later, through great good luck, I came to know the Abbey better and Michael and Alison Mayne with it. But, looking back, I see there were in that first meeting on that portentous evening elements which are characteristic of him and which recur again and again in this book.

Take, for instance, my reason for being at Westminster in the first place which was a literary one: this is a very literary book, shot through with references and quotations, the evidence of a lifetime's reading, quotations which I several times found myself cribbing and making my own note of. And the range is wide: this must surely be the first time that Martin Buber has shared a text with Jimmy Tarbuck.

That my poetry reading was in support of AIDS charities is typical too, as throughout his period in office Michael Mayne has consistently put the Abbey in the forefront of concern and response to the needs of victims, whether of disease or famine, discrimination or social injustice. It is a Christianity of rapid response, and as such is not to everybody's taste, particularly in a church that is at the heart of the Establishment. In an extract from his diary for December 1992 he tells of the spur of the moment decision to hold a carol service for 1600 miners and their families, who had come to London to demonstrate against the closing of the pits. The Grimethorpe Colliery Band played on the steps of the altar and the Bishop of Wakefield preached in a miner's helmet. There were services to mark the fifth anniversary of the Locherbie disaster, an ecumenical *Songs of Praise* during the Gulf War in which the senior Muslim joined hands with the Jewish Rabbi Hugo Gryn. There was a service of thanksgiving for the life of Bobby Moore and one for Les Dawson ... occasions guaranteed to send up the blood pressure of more traditionally minded Anglicans. Except that Michael Mayne is traditionally minded himself and one of the strengths of this book is the way he sets out the intellectual and theological reasoning behind his style of churchmanship and his stewardship at the Abbey.

Particularly illuminating in this connection are his remarks on the 'conflict between faithfulness to the Gospel and what the State expects of the Abbey as a church that (is) both established and "Establishment" '.

Palpable too on the tour he took me that evening in 1991 was the Dean's love for the fabric of the Abbey: as he talked about some of the recumbent effigies he would take their faces in both his hands out of sheer affection. That affection shines out from every chapter of this book, the learning worn lightly and linked very often to some contemporary occasion or extract from his diary . . . the actual form of the book, diary, reminiscence and devotional instruction a wonderfully readable mixture.

Finally there was our supper round the Aga and the homeliness of that, the ordinariness, is typical. He tells of trying in a lunch at the choir school to draw out a new eight-year-old choirboy; it was hard work and when the boy finally did utter it was to say, 'So, basically you're the Dean of Westminster'. Which of course is exactly what he did not feel he was, namely someone who identified solely with his office (and who would have been a much poorer priest had he done so). Vulnerable, approachable, he was ready, as one of his clerical detractors put it, 'to undress in public', the occasion of that particular criticism the publication of his account of being afflicted with ME during the year before he was appointed dean. The book he wrote about it has been a help and a comfort to many other sufferers from this mysterious condition, a malady so misunderstood that its very existence has been called into question.

Pray, Love, Remember is a Lenten book but it is not a dutiful read. The devotional instruction arises naturally from the record of Michael Mayne's ministry and is illuminated by it. As one who was brought up an Anglican and still feels emotionally drawn to the Church of England without now being a communicant I found the sections which deal with faith and intellectual honesty particularly relevant. I attended the farewell Eucharist which marked the Dean's retirement and though he doesn't talk about it in the book it was as remarkable as many of the occasions he records. The Abbey was packed, the congregation including some of the highest in the land and the lowliest, members of the Royal Family and the Government and men and women who slept in doorways. I remember sitting there as the congregation filed up to the altar steps to receive communion, feeling myself not able to go with them yet wanting to do so. I think, having read this book, I would perhaps be less intellectually fastidious and without forfeiting any integrity have felt able to join in.

Alan Bennett

Introduction

Thoroughbred dogs may win prizes at Cruft's, but mongrels are sometimes more appealing. And this is unashamedly a mongrel of a book. To be asked to write a 'Lent book' can feel like drawing the short straw. As a genus they often have about them a solemn austerity, and they may include suggested spiritual exercises arising from their weekly themes. But this is a book for Lent in only two senses: it is published well before Ash Wednesday, in the dying days of the previous year, and some may indeed opt to read it, bit by bit, during Lent; and each chapter is hung on the peg of the eight collects for Lent and Easter Day, singling out a handful of their implicit themes, themes that relate to our shared human journey. (Rather than Cranmer, or the new Church of England revised lectionary collects, I have opted for those from the widely used 1980 Alternative Service Book.)

Kafka said that a book should be an axe for the frozen sea within us, and this is also a very personal book – in my view, the only kind of book really worth writing – about the nature and significance for me of a place that over ten years became such a deeply valued part of my life: Westminster Abbey. Until 1986 the Abbey had been a remote, unconsidered building, last visited as a schoolboy, and if I had been asked how I saw it I should have muttered something about Coronations and 'the great and the good', and (pressed for adjectives) found it hard to choose between 'formal' and 'daunting'. In the past, it was sometimes undoubtedly just

that. Lord John Thynne, for example, was installed as a
Canon of Westminster in 1831 and remained until he died
in 1881.

Only to the Dean did Lord John give his whole hand; all others had
to be content with a gradually decreasing number of fingers
according to their position in the Collegiate Body.[1]

My first impression did little to destroy the illusion of somewhat grand protocol, for within ten days of my induction
as Dean I was taking part in the startling splendour and
pageantry of a royal wedding (that of the Duke and Duchess
of York); but when normality returned the building began
slowly to reveal itself and work its magic.

Writing of the Abbey a year after his retirement my pre-
decessor Edward Carpenter quoted the compliment paid by
Sir Richard Steele (the eighteenth-century founder of the
Spectator) to Lady Elizabeth Hastings: 'To love her is a liberal
education.'

Those who have come to know Westminster Abbey over long years
do not hesitate to resort to such language in expressing their deep
personal devotion to this great institution. This Collegiate Church
has watched, been part of and recorded a stirring national history.
To multitudes it has become the locus around which profound and
subliminal emotions cluster, registering those thoughts which break
through language and escape. Perhaps this is to be expected in a
building which has been prayed in, rejoiced in, wept in by kings
and commoners, saints and sinners over the centuries.[2]

Perhaps no other church in the world is at once so well
known and so little known, so charged with the sense of
nearly a thousand years of English history, so reflective of the
style and opinions of different ages, so walked through and
marvelled at; yet so little understood as a community that
is centred, as it has always been and always must be, on the

daily worship of God. At heart it is a body of people seeking to interpret their building to those who come into it as tourists or pilgrims, and to minister to those who wish to give thanks or remember, or who are hurt, troubled or perplexed.

'If the only prayer you say in your whole life is thank you,' wrote Meister Eckhart, 'that would suffice.' So this book is first and foremost a small act of deep gratitude to God: gratitude for the Abbey, for my former colleagues, and for the whole Abbey community. Included in each of the chapters are short relevant extracts from a diary kept spasmodically over these ten years, extracts that illustrate my theme and also something of the rich variety of the Abbey's life. Part of my purpose is to draw out certain unexpected aspects of the Abbey's multi-faceted ministry, and their implications for the life of the wider Church as it seeks to minister to people in all their mystery, in the wonder as well as the anguish of what it means to be human. But I hope it is also something more: an honest exploring of how these ten years have made me question my assumptions, and deepened some of my convictions, both about what we all have in common (searching, hungering, yearning, unfulfilled creatures that we are), and about the nature of the God in whose likeness each of us is made and who alone can satisfy us. And, above all, my convictions about that compelling story spelled out in these days of Lent, spelled out in the shared meal, in the two gardens in which the final drama is set and the desolation of that death on the cross that stands between them; and of how this story of God's self-giving love contains and unites all our lesser stories, and has the power to pull them together and make sense of them.

For it is that story which down the centuries has continued to resonate in people's lives, and which, once it has seized you, will not easily let you go.

ASH WEDNESDAY

The Tomb of the Unknown Warrior

On being human

Almighty and everlasting God,
you hate nothing that you have made
and forgive the sins of all those who are penitent.
Create and make in us new and contrite hearts,
that, lamenting our sins,
   and acknowledging our wretchedness,
we may receive from you, the God of all mercy,
perfect forgiveness and peace;
through Jesus Christ our Lord.

When on 6 September 1997 the body of Diana, Princess of Wales, was borne from Kensington Palace to lie before the High Altar of Westminster Abbey, the cortège arrived at the west door with miraculous precision, Big Ben striking the hour. It was a moment that exemplified the professionalism of the Services and the staff of the Royal Household, as well as that of a church that must be ready at any time to respond swiftly and with skilled expertise to the most unexpected events. Until this moment nothing stood in the way of the funeral cortège. But there is no route that lies straight as an arrow between door and altar, for it is interrupted by a grave. And so the eight men from the Welsh Guards who carried the lead coffin were forced to move slowly round the black marble stone, framed by scarlet poppies, that covers the tomb of an anonymous man. Though many Abbey graves are more outwardly imposing, this is the only one that no one ever walks over, as important as those of statesmen or monarchs. I shall return to it, and to the significance of that crooked route.

Sometimes I would watch from my study window overlooking the nave as people streamed though the doors in startling numbers. For much of the year they would come at the remarkable rate of 15,000 a day, people from diverse cultures and from every religious tradition and none. And I would reflect on the paradoxes that lie at the heart of the Abbey's daily life: the tension between welcome and control, pleasure that so many are drawn to its presence but anxiety for their safety in its constricted space; the tension, too, between the reality of a noisy, circulating mass of tourists and the ideal of a calm and peaceful atmosphere which allows breathing space in a 'place where prayer has been valid' for centuries; and I would reflect on how hard it is, in a building spinning daily with people from almost every nation upon earth, to communicate the truth of the unique and irreplaceable worth of each one of them.[1]

The Abbey means different things to different people: it is at once a medieval treasure-house, the Coronation church, a store-house of English history and the burial-place of thirty monarchs; but always first and foremost it is a living church, its primary task to worship God, to sing the daily offices and celebrate the Eucharist. What did we exist to offer these milling hordes who came, some as tourists, some as pilgrims, some to worship, some to stare, yet each one of them experiencing certain moments at which teasing questions need to be faced? Not the 'how?' questions that increasingly science can answer, but the 'why?' questions of philosophy, literature and religion about the point of it all; and not just the bewildered middle-of-the-night questions, but also questions that arise from our longing to love and be loved, our need to forgive and be forgiven, our desire to understand and be understood, our yearning to be at peace with each other and within ourselves. Those yearnings do not vanish

2

in those for whom the structures of faith are drained of meaning, those who continue to surprise 'a hunger in themselves to be more serious'.[2] So what kind of a God might they glimpse, those who chose to attend one of the four daily acts of worship, through our liturgy, our preaching and our music? What kind of a community might they perceive through the way in which we welcomed them, even in such overwhelming numbers; or in the sensitivity and discretion with which we chose to speak with this or that person in need, or simply let them be, each contained in his or her chosen privacy?

The answers, such as they are, lie in the pages of this book. Yet the questions all arise from that pivotal understanding of what it means to be a human being. Ash Wednesday is a day for honesty, a realistic assessment of the human heart. By tradition it is a day when we reassert (unfashionably but rightly) the sinfulness of our nature, and ask God to '**create and make in us new and contrite hearts**', and many kneel to have ash placed on their foreheads in the shape of a cross. But even in the stringent days of Lent there is a complementary truth which also needs affirming. We may be dust, but we are dust that is full of mystery and that dreams of glory; dust (we sense) that is to be changed, transfigured, into God's own likeness.

A sixth-century church historian, Evagrius, described sin as 'forgetfulness of God's goodness', a forgetfulness of his purpose in creating us, a forgetfulness that causes us time and time again to betray ourselves and each other. Blind to our true potential and turned in upon ourselves, we are capable (as is evident daily) of damaging both others and ourselves by acts which range through trivial thoughtlessness to ones of unspeakable cruelty, aggression and violence. Yet the genuine anguish we may then feel and the sense that this is not how things should be, or the stirrings of compassion we experience in the face of another's need and our response to goodness when we meet it, these witness to something quite different.

When I ask what it means to be human I have to answer that it means being a unique chemical mix fused with an equally unique and irreplaceable spirit; that to be a human being is to be an embodied spirit, conscious (even if only in rare moments) of that 'sense of beyondness at the heart of things'. I know – though it is more instinct than knowledge and I am forced to use words which are slippery and imprecise – that in the depth of myself, in stillness, I am aware of some 'other' that is not me, and yet is the very ground of my existence. Sometimes Christians speak and write as if they alone possess a privileged insight into what it means to be human. In our churches we readily employ an exclusive kind of language that only the enlightened will understand. Yet every human being is made in the image of God and has that which is of God within them. Augustine and Meister Eckhart and the author of *The Cloud of Unknowing* and Teresa of Avila knew this, as did poets like Traherne and Hopkins: for them God not only pervades the whole universe as the ultimate source of its life, but is present in every soul, and can be responded to by love by every human being who really desires to know and respond to him. ('You spare all things because they are yours, O Lord, who love all that lives; for your imperishable breath is in every one.'³) What Christians claim – and it is a radical claim – is that they have a different frame of reference, one that draws on a God whose nature was once and is for ever revealed in one, unique, definitive and fully human life, and that in Jesus the full force of what it is to be human is newly defined. He enables us to see with changed eyes, to look at both world and neighbour and perceive (to use Martin Buber's terms) that everything is Thou and nothing is It. In W. H. Auden's Christmas oratorio *For the Time Being* the three Wise Men who have come in search of the Christ-child say:

> To discover how to be human now
> Is the reason we follow this star.

All are called to become human in the truest and fullest meaning of that word.

Nor is it simply what we too narrowly define as 'religious' experience that is grounded in our shared humanity. Edward Robinson, in his book *The Language of Mystery*, writes:

How is it that we recognise authority in *King Lear*, in *Cancer Ward* and in the *Glagolithic Mass*? Not because of any experience we have of ancient Britain, of the Soviet camps, or of Bohemian folk music, but because at the deeper level of our common humanity Shakespeare and Solzhenitsyn and Janáček all speak to us of something we already know, however dimly. Somewhere inside us an echo, a resonance is stirred; something in each of us says 'yes'. If these figures speak with authority, it is because they are like us, in sharing our humanity, yet also unlike, in having something that we want; something we can use, something we can appropriate, something that could perhaps help us to become the people we have it in us to become.[4]

And Seamus Heaney, when he is analysing the need the poet has to write, describes how first he appeases that need by learning to find his own unique and distinctive voice, but

then begins a bothersome and exhilarating second need, to go beyond himself and take on the otherness of the world in works that remain his own *yet offer rights-of-way to everybody else* [my italics] . . . What poets do is to encourage our inclination to credit the promptings of our intuitive being. They help us to say in the recesses of ourselves . . . 'Yes, I know something like that too . . . Yes, that's right. Thank you for putting words on it and making it more or less official'.[5]

It is as if writers and artists and musicians, in sharing their vision, are enabling us to respond to what is in fact the true grain of the universe, exposing us to at least a hint of the meaning we search and long for. John Bowden writes:

Scientists, moral philosophers and artists, as well as religious believers, have spoken of their discovery that the relationship between man and reality is somehow a two-way one, of such a kind as to produce an echo, a resonance – and not a bad definition of religion is to term it that sphere in which our sensitivity to this resonance . . . is increased. Suppose we believe we are called to the vision of God, and in pursuit of that vision are also called to love, reconciliation, forgiveness and the achievement of freedom, the enhancement of life, the search for and creation of beauty, because that is what we are made for . . . must we not argue that we believe . . . this because it is true, rather than just because it is Christian?[6]

True, because it fits the mould in which we are cast. Many who have spent time listening with real attention to another person in need will know that frequently we find in others the familiar echo of what we know in ourselves: a deep, unsatisfied desire. It is, I believe, a kind of homesickness, a longing for the bringing to fruition of that potential for love and those natural springs of compassion that help define our humanity. The beginning and end of compassion is a question of how we see: how you see me, how I see you. This need that we share, to be seen, to be noticed and given value, is not some childish craving for attention: it is the only way we have to become our true selves. Egos are lonely, and egotism a lonely way of being, and our spirits are fed by what we freely give each other. It is not only babies who languish and grow sick if they are starved of love. I am affirmed when you notice me, when you give me your attention. However old we grow, however wise, the child we once were is always part of us and, in one way or another, every human being (far less confident than we appear, most of us)

6

cries out or acts out – or often, disastrously stifles – their need to be recognised, perhaps forgiven, but most often simply encouraged: to know that 'you matter because you are you'.[7] And we are so bad at it. Only last night an OFSTED inspector told me that recently she was at an inner-city school, a struggling, bottom-of-the-league-tables sort of school, where there was a West Indian woman teacher who was a shining exception to the rest. She took her aside and told her what a great teacher she was, at which the woman broke down in tears of gratitude, because 'no one has ever told me that before'.

One day the poet W. B. Yeats was out walking when he had one of those small epiphanies – those rare but unforgettable moments of sudden clear perception – that enable us to see some truth with new eyes.

I was walking . . . over the bit of marshy ground close to Inchy Wood when there swept over me a sense of dependence on a great personal Being somewhere far off yet near at hand, and I heard a voice speaking to me saying, 'No human soul is like any other human soul, and therefore the love of God for any human soul is infinite, *for no other soul can satisfy the same need in God*'[8] (my italics).

Martin Buber shares that belief and distinguishes between 'egos' and 'persons':

Egos appear by setting themselves apart from other egos. *Persons* appear by entering into relation to other persons . . . Each soul stands in the splendour of its own existence. In each person there is something precious that is in no other person.[9]

The poet who has a passionate concern with the unique individuality of every living thing is Gerard Manley Hopkins, with his theory of 'inscape' and 'instress'. The first relates to the quintessential identity of each thing, its particularity as itself and not another thing, the absolute *thisness*-and-not-thatness of it; the second to the power (namely, of God) that keeps that individuality in being. In 'As Kingfishers Catch Fire', he writes of how

> Each mortal thing does one thing and the same:
> ... myself it speaks and spells,
> Crying What I do is me: for that I came[10]

When we are children it is the separate integrity of each thing on earth that delights us – the fact that a snail is a snail and not a beetle – and this recognition is also the beginning of ethics, since such a perception ought to lead to the realisation that each person on earth is unique, too, and should be treated that way. I am uniquely me and not you; you are uniquely you and not me, the self we have always been and always will be.

Which brings me back to my question of how, in all the frenetic activity of the Abbey's daily life, we sought to witness to the truth that every single human being, even the brassiest gum-chewing, T-shirted, travel-weary tourist, 'stands each in the splendour of its own existence' and is of unique worth in the sight of God. And why those eight Welsh Guardsmen had to take a crooked route as they conveyed the coffin containing the mortal remains of Diana, Princess of Wales, from the west door to the high altar.

It was in October 1920 that an Army chaplain, The Reverend David Railton, wrote to the then dean suggesting that the body of an unidentified soldier should be dug up from among the hundreds of thousands of corpses still lying in the soil of the battlefields where their bodies had been roughly covered with earth, and brought home to lie in the Abbey to represent the millions of British and Commonwealth servicemen who had died fighting in the Great War.

Dean Ryle put the idea to King George V. That very conservative monarch found the proposal worrying.

His Majesty is inclined to think [wrote his Private Secretary] that nearly two years after the last shot was fired on the battlefields of France and Flanders is so long ago that a funeral now might be regarded as belated, and almost, as it were, reopen the war wound which time is gradually healing.[11]

But the dean persisted and won the enthusiastic support of Lloyd George, so the king reluctantly agreed. The military authorities were asked to exhume six unidentified bodies from under their rough crosses marked 'unknown' in the battlefields of Belgium and northern France. Each was placed in a plain deal coffin and laid in a hut not far from Ypres. They then blindfolded a young British officer, Henry Williams (who died only in 1993, aged 96), and led him inside. The first body he touched was chosen, and taken to Boulogne. There it was placed in a plain coffin made from a Hampton Court oak, and sealed with two great straps, under which was placed a ceremonial sword given by the now enthusiastic king. The ceremonial for the service was in the hands of a Cabinet committee under Lord Curzon. In the words of Ronald Blythe:

[Curzon] – who had stopped to observe a platoon of naked Tommies bathing in the sea and had remarked, 'How is it that I have never been informed that the lower orders had such white skins?' – was to stage state obsequies for a farm labourer, an apprentice, a clerk – though just possibly a peer.[12]

On the journey from Victoria, as the cortège attended by Field Marshals and Admirals passed by, the large crowds stood silent. For the funeral a hundred VCs lined the nave. The king was the chief mourner. *The Times* described the service as 'the most beautiful, the most touching and the most impressive . . . this island has ever seen.' Afterwards, at 11 p.m. when the doors were finally closed to the thousands of people who had come to pay tribute, the grave was filled in with a hundred sandbags of soil brought from all the countries where allied troops had fought – just as, eight hundred years before, soil had been brought from the Holy Land for the foundations of the Shrine of Edward the Confessor. In the following year a black marble gravestone from Belgium was laid over it. Within a week of the funeral service a million people had visited the grave and a hundred thousand wreaths had been laid at the Cenotaph. As with that other funeral service in the Abbey 77 years later, it provided a focus for a public outpouring of grief, a sense of release, a ritual that gave people permission to grieve for the loss of those they loved, those private griefs which nevertheless may need a public expression which until that moment they had lacked.

In my ten years at the Abbey I welcomed an impressive number of heads of state who, on a visit to London, come at once to lay a wreath at the foot of the grave of that nameless, classless, ageless man, who has become more famed than all the great and the good who lie around him, and who has come to represent the much wider constituency of those who have died in the wars of our century. Standing there on these and other more poignant occasions, and invariably during the silence on Remembrance Sunday, I would try to imagine him during the long, idyllic summer of 1914, or living in the foul stench of the fetid trenches; try to imagine what George Steiner calls 'the tear in the fabric of natural life caused by the fact that this man will have fathered no children, known no grandchildren, and that by [his] early death we remain deprived.'[13] And I would think of Auden's lines:

> To save your world, you asked this man to die:
> Would this man, could he see you now, ask why?[14]

10

Over the years I came to understand that this was much more than just another war memorial. For it is saying that every single casualty in war was someone's son or father, husband or lover, and that each death, each war office telegram, each official letter of sympathy, was heart-breaking. In honouring this one anonymous man and placing him in this most public part of the Abbey on Remembrance Day 1920 they were making the strongest possible statement about human value; about the worth of every single human being. We in our turn were affirming that truth. We were saying that we have no right to call anyone 'ordinary', for each one of us is extraordinary, an ensouled body made in the divine likeness; and the real blindness, that culpable blindness of the spirit that can only be compared to living in the dark, is the failure to see the true value, the wonder and the mystery of every person you meet.

I came to see that there is a further truth to be understood. I am told that this is the only national war memorial in the world that stands within a Christian church. By its presence here it affirms that this man's story is linked to a much greater story. When the Gulf War began in 1990 we threw a spotlight on the Grave of the Unknown Warrior and placed in front of it a large bronze crucifix, so that as people entered the Abbey they saw the grave in the shadow of the man hanging on a cross. And that was our way of saying, to those with eyes to see: Christians don't believe in a God who is remote and indifferent to his creatures and their suffering, but in one who so loves his creation that he reveals his nature in the only language we can understand, in the human language of one man's birth, life, suffering and cruel death. It is not that the death of a soldier in war can in any way be equated with that death on Calvary; it is rather what this other life and death disclose of the God who fails to answer our agonised questions about the why? of pain and suffering and loss, but instead (in that most profound of

11

mysteries) himself enters into the questions. And in doing so gives them a quite new frame of reference.

None of us is immune to pain. We get sick; we die. We lose those who mean most to us in the world. There is no such thing as divine protection. Jesus died an agonising death. So what did he die to prove? He died to prove the seemingly foolish claim that the self-giving love that shaped his own life is what lies at the creative heart of the universe; and that if you would name the unimaginable presence that informs it and holds it in being, then you must use the name 'Abba', the intimate name a child gives its father. And that life is about learning to trust that these things are so; and learning to grow in that same self-giving love.

Remembrance Sunday 1990

The timing has to be immaculate. With Big Ben on our doorstep striking the hour for the 11 o'clock silence, the service must have reached exactly the right point. Both nave and quire are full, the former partly made up of young servicemen and women. After the psalm and anthem, the readings and the prayers, we move in procession to the nave, three senior officers bringing up the rear, and gather around the Unknown Warrior's Grave. As the hymn ends I say a brief prayer of remembrance; then at 10.55.15 the choir sings the haunting Russian 'Kontakion for the Departed'. As the last note dies away, Big Ben begins to strike, in the distance a gun is fired, and the Abbey is enfolded in a profound silence.

There follow the Last Post and the Reveille, and then – for all with war-time memories – one of those moments that send a shiver down your spine and which you know will lodge, burr-like, in your mind. For standing beside the Abbey Choir this morning is a second one: 90 young people from Dresden, members of the *Kreutzhcor* under their aged conductor. Both choirs sing together 'Blessed are the Dead' from Brahms' *Requiem*; and my mind goes back to the horror that was the saturation bombing of Dresden a mere three months before the end of the war, and to Bishop George Bell who so angered Churchill by denouncing in the House of Lords such apparently meaningless destruction: 100,000 German civilians killed in a single February night, many by burning or choking to death in the firestorm. The young people are the grandchildren and great-grandchildren of those who suffered those horrors and may not fully grasp, as the old man conducting them surely does, the significance of this reconciling moment. After the war the German church leaders, in the Stuttgart Declaration, said: 'With great pain do we say that through us great suffering has been brought upon many peoples and lands. We ask for forgiveness.' I wish that the spirit of George Bell had prevailed and that the British Churches in their turn had asked forgiveness of the German people for such events as the saturation bombing of Dresden.

17 December 1992

Hundreds of miners and their wives and children from the Wake-field area have arrived in London for a peaceful, though forceful, demonstration against the Government's rigid policy of closing vir-tually all the pits, which will result in widespread unemployment and a consequent sense of being devalued. At very short notice we decide to hold a carol service for 1600 of them. By our support as the church most closely identified with 'the Establishment', we are not so much commenting on Government policy as on the heartless manner in which the virtual closing down of one of Britain's for-merly great industries is being achieved.

The service is amazing. Grimethorpe Colliery Band plays seated on the steps of the high altar. Twenty children carry up in procession what they have called 'symbols of hope'. They include miners' lamps and helmets, models of pit derricks, a birthday cake with 31 candles on it – there are 31 pits being forcibly closed – and a lump of coal. The Bishop of Wakefield gives an address wearing a miner's helmet, for once a justified gimmick. Afterwards, hundreds stay and mingle around the Unknown Warrior at the back of the nave, Cardinal Basil Hume talking to Arthur Scargill, the Bishop of London to a group of miners' children. Later, I am presented with a lamp from Grimethorpe Colliery, and I shall prize it. For it will be a reminder of a powerful occasion in which the Abbey has been used to meet a real community need, and in so doing to witness to the truth about human value.

Almighty and everlasting God,
you hate nothing that you have made . . .
for the whole creation proclaims your marvellous work,
and you have fashioned each one of us in your own image.
Create and make in us new and contrite hearts,
that seeing each other with enlightened eyes
and knowing our proper value in your sight,
we may receive from you, the God of all mercy,
perfect forgiveness and peace;
through Jesus Christ our Lord.

2

LENT I

St Faith's Chapel

On being tempted; and on prayer

Almighty God,
whose Son Jesus Christ fasted forty days in the wilderness,
and was tempted as we are, yet without sin:
give us grace to discipline ourselves
   in obedience to your Spirit;
and, as you know our weakness,
so may we know your power to save;
through Jesus Christ our Lord.

The poet e. e. cummings – ever insistent on the use of the lower case except for 'God' – has a poem about a small country church whose

> prayers are prayers of earth's own clumsily striving
> (finding and losing and laughing and crying)children
> whose any sadness and joy is my grief or my gladness
>
> around me surges a miracle of unceasing
> birth and glory and death and resurrection:
> over my sleeping self float flaming symbols
> · of hope,and i wake to a perfect patience of mountains . . .
>
> winter by spring,i lift my diminutive spire to
> merciful Him Whose only now is forever:
> standing erect in the deathless truth of His presence
> (welcoming humbly His light and proudly His darkness)[1]

15

Forget the mountains and the 'diminutive spire', and the words perfectly capture the timelessness of every place consecrated to the God 'Whose only now is forever', places that exist in order to serve

earth's own clumsily striving
(finding and losing and laughing and crying)children
whose any sadness and joy is my grief or my gladness

As the time drew near for me to leave the Abbey, the building that I had watched in all its varying moods, celebratory and solemn, I began to observe it with new attention. I loved to look down the full length of the quire and nave from my seat in the sanctuary, perhaps during some less-than-gripping sermon or address, and watch the play of light, especially on a clear day in spring or autumn when the sun was low, as it fell on the richly decorated organ cases on the quire screen and on the narrow, graceful arches of the long, vaulted, fan-like roof, patchily turning the stone from grey to amber. At the far end there was the hint of scarlet poppies around that unknown man's grave, echoed beyond the glass doors by the red Tour of London buses trawling for prey in Victoria Street. I thought of Edward the Confessor deciding in 1043 to rebuild the small monastic church in Reigate stone and on a scale that would eclipse anything seen in England before; and of Henry III pulling down Edward's church two hundred years later so that the present Abbey might replace it, again building on an unrivalled scale of Gothic splendour. It cost the king nearly £50,000, almost twice the Crown's annual income. To the King's Quay on the Thames came boatloads of ragstone from Kent and from Caen, tin from Cornwall, Purbeck marble from Dorset, lead from Derbyshire, and timber from the king's forests in Essex. To build on a scale of such magnificence and with such exquisite detail was the best way they knew of acknowledging and honouring the sovereignty of God. I thought of how the space they created within the slender columns and curving arches was then scored by history and began to tell the story of the English people. It was fashioned by the powerful forces of monasticism, by the Reformation and the Commonwealth; and it slowly filled up with the tombs of monarchs and the graves and often idiosyncratic tombs and memorials of those who shaped our national life: the poets, novelists and scientists, the soldiers and the statesmen.

Sometimes, walking around the Abbey at night – a strangely benign space, despite the four thousand or so bodies buried under foot and long since turned to dust – I thought of the men and women whose stories are part of its own story, for it is a *peopled* space. This has been the place which has witnessed for centuries the great landmarks on the human journey, all acted out in what Philip Larkin calls this

> serious house on serious earth.
> In whose blent air all our compulsions meet,
> Are recognised, and robed as destinies.[2]

In his autobiography the historian G. M. Trevelyan writes:

Once, on this earth, once, on this familiar spot of ground, walked other men and women, as actual as we are today, thinking their own thoughts, swayed by their own passions, but now all gone, one generation vanishing after another, gone as utterly as we ourselves shall shortly be gone like ghosts at cockcrow.[3]

But the memories remain: of Richard II felling the Earl of Arundel with one stroke of a verger's mace when the earl arrived late for the night-time funeral of Richard's beloved queen, Anne of Bohemia; of the young Henry V coming to the Abbey in simple dress to share in the great service of thanksgiving after the Battle of Agincourt; of Cromwell's soldiers removing the stained glass and smashing up the organ and pawning its pipes; of Samuel Pepys, taken short during the coronation of Charles II; of Samuel Johnson weeping at the burial in Poets' Corner of his dear friend the actor David Garrick, who had ridden down from Lichfield beside him to seek their respective livings and who now lie side by side in death; of William Blake climbing on the monuments in order to draw the figures more accurately; of Charles Dickens being buried secretly, in the presence of a handful of mourners, early on a morning in June; of Thomas Hardy, his ashes buried here in 1928 beside Dickens, his heart in a Dorset churchyard – and a memory of celebrating the 150th anniversary of his birth when a young Dorset musician stood over his grave and played 'The Rosebud in Summer' on Hardy's own violin.

And all the while, through the Black Death, the Wars of the Roses and the Hundred Years War, through the religious turmoil that saw the birth of the Church of England and the political turmoil that was the Civil War, through the Age of Enlightenment and the seeming bombshell of Darwinism (though Darwin is now rightly buried in the nave), through the long age of Empire and its metamorphosis into the Commonwealth, through the Blitz and into our own troubled century, the Abbey has remained faithful to its original and primary purpose. For the Confessor, as for Henry Plantagenet, there was no mistaking that purpose: it was to do the Opus Dei, the daily work of God, to sing the divine offices and to celebrate Mass. The Benedictine rule that ordered the life of the monastery saw daily life as all of a piece: worship and daily work and feeding the hungry, clothing the naked and welcoming the stranger, were inseparable; they could not be divided into that which is of God and that which is not. Their daily life and work were not so much interrupted by, as contained within and stitched together by those seven offices and the daily Mass. And the great monastic abbeys and churches were built in order that the Opus

Dei might be done, not just with care and devotion, but aided by all the richness of architecture, all the subtlety of colour and ceremonial, all the beauty of words and music, of which we human beings are capable when we approach God – or, rather, when we consciously open ourselves to his presence in our midst. And those who built our churches created spaces intended to arouse in those who entered them a sense of entering a special space, evoking that sense of awe which is the beginning of worship. A space in which the offering of the Opus Dei, day in, day out, year in, year out, for centuries, has created a kind of holy rhythm that has invaded the very stones.

This is why those of us responsible for ordering the Abbey's life tried never to forget that it is not just a peopled space – a desperately busy and over-peopled space – but a sacred space, a place whose chief task, the worship of God, has never changed, nor ever can. God is omnipresent, the very source of our life, and yet we need churches, as we need the Eucharist, to focus the reality of that presence. And what churches are for is to provide the space in which we human beings may seek to traffic with the transcendent, to become aware of, and respond to, a presence which is beyond us, both greater and other than we are. We sought to meet the needs of individuals and communities in imaginative, empathetic ways (and I shall be writing of some of them), but nothing mattered more than the quality of our worship and the care and thoughtfulness we brought to ordering the space we had to fill. Nothing was more important than the act of worship that began each day or the Evensong, so beautifully sung by the choir six times a week, that ended it. On a bleak November evening, say, when for the space of forty minutes those seemingly timeless words of scripture, psalm, anthem and prayers, brought us back to the reality that underlies those daily unrealities that threaten to take over our lives. It was as if they contained the day, contained it between these two steady poles, and after the often frenetic busy-ness of the packed church, the building seemed to sigh and settle for the night. And each Sunday, as the hundreds of visitors – from every Christian tradition and none – flooded out of the Eucharist, many would say it was an experience they would not easily forget, meaning (I believe) that the music, the liturgy and the beauty and ambience of the spacious building had succeeded in taking them out of themselves, even to glimpse some truth about the love of God, or of their own mystery.

But the Abbey is not just a single space, but many, and for me the daily praying heart of the Abbey was not the nave or the quire, nor even St Edward's Shrine, where the body of the saint still lies (though that is indeed a uniquely prayerful space), but a small chapel tucked away behind a stout medieval door at the end of Poets' Corner. It was here that up to a dozen of us began each day, first with a time of corporate silence shortly after 7 a.m., then with morning prayer at 7.30, followed by the Eucharist at 8 o'clock. It is a chapel whose east wall is covered with a thirteenth-century painting of St Faith, a small self-portrait of the Benedictine monk who painted her to one side of her; a place whose walls are so thick that there is always an extraordinary quality of silence. Here people can drop in at any time of the day to sit or kneel to say their prayers: to explore (in whatever way suits them best) that other, more important inner space unique to each one of us.

I have called this book *Pray, Love, Remember*, taking the words from Shakespeare, who once (allegedly) stood just outside the door into St Faith's Chapel at the burial of his fellow-poet Edmund Spenser, and whose memorial now stands there. Ophelia, driven mad by her treatment at the hands of Hamlet, comes before Claudius, Gertrude and Laertes with herbs and flowers. 'There's rosemary', she says to Laertes, 'that's for remembrance; pray, love, remember.' And it struck me how well those three words describe the heart of the Christian life, which is to pray, to love and (in the eucharistic sense) to remember. I guess I have never doubted the primacy of prayer, though I've often ignored it and still find it hard, sometimes wearisome, to practise it. Looking back, I can see that there has been a journey of sorts, and with certain distinctive milestones, though it has often felt more like exploring a maze with its frequent dead ends than following a well-trodden path. At times, like R. S. Thomas, I have felt like one who throws

> gravel
> at the sky's
> window, hoping to attract
> the loved one's
> attention
> [and who would have]
> refrained long since
> but that peering once
> through my locked fingers
> I thought that I detected
> the movement of a curtain.[4]

Or again, like one who leans

> far out
> over an immense depth, letting
> (God's) name go and waiting,
> somewhere between faith and doubt,
> for the echoes of its arrival.[5]

Few find faith easy. 'There is a would-be believer in every unbeliever; an agnostic in every church-goer.'[6] Faith is not absolute certainty, but a readiness to explore the Mystery. It is not a method of finding all the answers, but of living with the questions. Like hope, it is an attitude of mind, an orientation of the spirit. Doubt is part of faith, not its rejection, an honest refusal to be prematurely convinced, and

'Christianity an offered answer to the human quest for meaning; an invitation to explore life in the light of the Christian interpretation' of it.[7]

Nor is prayer easy. In a sense priests should count themselves lucky. Praying – at least in public – is part of the job. There is a rubric in the Preface to Cranmer's Book of Common Prayer which directs Anglican clergy to say the offices of morning and evening prayer daily 'either privately or openly, not being let by sickness, or some other urgent cause'. Over the years 'urgent causes' can cover a multitude of sins, and the offices can get crowded out of a tight schedule and even become a chore. Leading worship is part of a priest's job, but that may become counter-productive so far as your own inner prayer life is concerned. For I'm not speaking of those professional tasks of conducting services, celebrating the eucharist, leading intercessions, praying with the sick, but of that primary Christian duty laid upon every baptised person: the regular setting aside of a space in one's life in order to give attention to God. That is what I have sometimes ignored.

I think of racing round my large and demanding parish in the 1960s, busier than I had ever been, doing all those thousand-and-one things my over-active conscience urged upon me, visiting the sick and the old and the newcomer, writing sermons, administering, planning, setting up prayer groups, counselling individuals – yet often ignoring the one thing necessary: creating a daily space in which to explore what Jeremy Taylor spoke of when he said that

There should be in the soul halls of space, avenues of leisure and high porticos of silence, where God waits.[8]

Then in the seventies I worked for seven years in the BBC as Head of Radio Religious Programmes. I was attached to a local church at weekends, but battled my way to London daily on British Rail stock that was on its last legs, always dirty and crowded, usually late, arriving home harassed and weary; and I kidded myself that it was enough to lead a fortnightly prayer group and somewhat half-heartedly intercede for my family and any in special need as I tramped down Great Portland Street each morning to Broadcasting House. It wasn't – and in my heart I knew it. From there I went to Great St Mary's, the University Church in Cambridge, another demanding, often draining job; yet it was there that I learned (at least some of the time) to put prayer back in its rightful place, and it was like rediscovering one's proper habitat. We remodelled a small chapel and gave it a visual focus, a sculpted figure of the risen Christ, and provided a number of prayer stools; and then set aside the thirty minutes each day before evensong for corporate silence. And when, after seven years, I moved to the Abbey, the early morning stillness of St Faith's Chapel became the most valued space in the day.

How we pray, indeed whether we pray, depends first and last on our understanding of God; and in particular on whether we understand two things: that God has been revealed as Christ-like; and that we cannot remove ourselves from the One 'in whom we live and move and have our being' any more than we can from the air that surrounds us and fills our lungs. By the very fact that I exist I am in the presence of God: if I was not, I should cease to be a human being. It is as simple as that. That remarkable thirteenth-century Dominican friar and mystic Meister Eckhart writes of how it is necessary, if we are to be persons in the fullest sense, to become aware of what he called 'a transcendent abyss' within ourselves which only God can fill; of how God has an infinite capacity for giving, and each human soul an infinite capacity for receiving; of how the deepest mystery about us is that we can find God in the depth of ourselves, and having begun to do so we can then begin to find him everywhere. 'Our whole business in life', writes St Augustine, 'is to restore to health the eye and the heart whereby God may be seen.'[9] 'Though God be everywhere', writes William Law, 'yet he is present to thee in the deepest and most central part of the soul.'[10] That is the primary, given reality: the relationship which we may deny or ignore, but out of which we cannot fall, and all our little acts of prayer – our vocal prayers, our times of meditation, or that prayer of simple, loving attention we call contemplation – all these are secondary: conscious reminders of whom we are and whose we are. For prayer is not an escape from life, a few minutes cut out of life, but a regular, disciplined reminder that all life is lived in God's presence, a marvelling at God's love as that is shown in Christ, a thankful responding to that transcendent reality by whom we are held in being.

Prayer, then, is not primarily something I do in order to achieve something, but something I do because this is the sort of creature I am called to be: one who has an intuitive sense of the transcendent, a muffled but persistent sense of the presence of the holy. This is the way God in Christ calls me to realise my true potential as a child of God. Which is why in my third year at the Abbey I proposed that once a year, on a Saturday, we should close the Abbey to all visitors and tourists for an ecumenical day of prayer, a day of teaching and learning, of theory and practice, thereby affirming our primary purpose as a church, and encouraging people to explore together the activity that is at once the most natural and the most difficult. Hundreds came annually, and an annual tradition was established which still continues.

3 March 1992

This year's Day of Prayer is led by that holy and wise man, Archbishop Antony Bloom, the Russian Orthodox Archbishop in London. Disgruntled Japanese tourists find notices on the west gate – and courteous marshals – informing them that the Abbey is closed: people are praying. Or rather, learning how to do it a bit better. At the east end, ranged along the altar steps, are rows of candles and two fine Taizé icons. By 10 a.m. nearly four hundred people have come, from many different traditions, and after the welcome we have a short act of worship with readings and Taizé chants. There are two plenary sessions, morning and afternoon, and between them we divide people into groups of 15, each with its prayer leader, all of whom came last night for a short training session. The groups are scattered throughout the Abbey, and spend 45 minutes in a gently assisted time of contemplative silence. Some choose an object – an icon, a candle – as the focus on which to centre the attention; others use an incident from the gospels; yet others prefer a word or a phrase – 'Abba', perhaps, or 'Christ be with me' – or the Jesus Prayer. Before the final act of worship there is a question session in which Archbishop Antony tackles many of the familiar, probing anxieties about the how? and why? of prayer that have tantalised human beings for centuries, and will continue to do so to the end of time.

I guess the proper weighing of *being* and *doing* in our lives, and the priority we are ready to give to prayer, is the hardest challenge and the most consistent testing of the seriousness of our readiness to follow Christ. The man who taught me much about faithfulness in prayer was my colleague at Great St Mary's Giles Ecclestone, who was to die far too young of a rapid cancer a few years later. And it was his father, that remarkable parish priest Alan Ecclestone, who once said that 'the work of Christ consisted in his obedience to, his unswerving trust in, the Silence he called Father'.[11] Nothing about the ministry of Jesus is more striking than his stead-fast, undeviating openness to the Father, the times of withdrawal for uninterrupted prayer, that absolute depen-dence which enabled St John to speak of him as 'the one who is closest to the Father's heart' and which makes the cry of desolation from the cross all the more awesome.

In this first full week of Lent the collect asserts that Jesus **was tempted as we are, yet without sin,** and the Gospel reading (in most churches) tells of that testing that came to him in the wilderness. (The word 'temptation', which appears 21 times in the New Testament, only once denotes 'temptation to sin'; here it means 'trial, testing, ordeal'.) These tales of stones which might be turned into bread, of the view from the pinnacle of the temple, a vision of earthly power, and of putting God to the test by leaping from a high mountain, are stories both about Jesus' acceptance of his mission and of the manner in which it is to be achieved. And, as George Caird points out, the test comes at the points of his greatest strengths: his compassion (why not turn stones into bread both for his own needs, and also to win over the hungry crowds?); his commitment (why not take the popular way and become the political Messiah leading a war of liberation?); and his faith (if you really trust the Father, then what can harm you?).[12] He was to be tested in these three ways throughout his short ministry with insistent demands upon his compassion; by the enthusiasm that longed to make him a national hero; and by the scepticism that demanded a sign from heaven. All of it reaching a climax in that final mocking cry: 'If you are the King of the Jews, save yourself!'

I have always known those tests as real temptations, and quite often failed to resist them. The constant temptation to let prayer slip. The temptation, when I do pray, to pray narrowly and selfishly for my own needs. The temptation to go along with the crowd, to be popular at all costs, to meet people's (often quite invalid) expectations; and the equally invalid and immature assumption on my own part that God will protect me from those overwhelming blows that life, in all its unpredictability, can deliver. We find it hard to grasp the truth that when each of us is equally loved by God, yet set to live within the dangerous context of freedom, God can have no favourites. And certainly there could be no better setting in which to learn the two cardinal lessons of our life: how to love and how to trust. Which is why I am claiming that the priority we are willing to give to the deepening of that relationship with God we call prayer is the most consistent testing of the seriousness of our readiness to follow Christ. For it reveals what we most deeply desire.

'Lord, teach us to pray', his friends had said to Jesus. And what he does is not simply to tell them how to pray but to give them a prayer that will form a bond of unity between them and between all Christians ever after, a kind of recognisable watermark of authenticity, all we shall ever need to express our trusting, dependent relationship with God. As Simone Weil wrote:

The Our Father contains all possible petitions . . . It is impossible to say it once through, giving the fullest possible attention to each word, without a change, however infinitesimal perhaps, but real, taking place in the soul.[13]

Whether we use the Lord's Prayer, or some other inwardly repeated words, the constant repetition day in and day out, year in and year out, to help us focus down and to lead us into stillness, is not a debasing of the coinage. Quite the reverse. For as the familiar words sink down from the mind into the heart they become the means, at any point of the day or night, of instantly recalling that relationship in which we stand with the Christ-like God, whose love for us will always exceed anything we can begin to conceive or ever, in this life, understand.

Almighty God,
whose Son Jesus Christ fasted forty days and forty nights
    in the wilderness,
and was tempted as we are, yet without sin:
we thank you for the holy places that have spoken to us of
    your presence;

help us to guard the inner space in our lives
by keeping faithful to our life of prayer;
give us grace to discipline ourselves
   in obedience to your Spirit;
and, as you know our weakness,
so may we know your power to save;
through Jesus Christ our Lord.

3

LENT II

The Nave and Quire

On valid and invalid expectations;
on role-playing and integrity

**Lord God Almighty,
grant your people grace
to withstand the temptations
   of the world, the flesh and the devil,
and with pure hearts and minds
to follow you, the only God;
through Jesus Christ our Lord.**

20 October 1989

We hold Laurence Olivier's Memorial Service on a golden autumn day, the same day on which Sir Henry Irving was buried in Poet's Corner 84 years ago. The Abbey congregation of two thousand is like an illustration for *Who's Who in the Theatre*. It is – it has to be – a very theatrical event, an act of worship, thanksgiving and remembrance hand-crafted to the man who was so consummate an actor. Following William Walton's *Fanfare* composed for the film of *Hamlet*, we process to 'Praise to the Holiest in the height'. Behind Prince Edward and the royal representatives come the actors, each bearing an item symbolic of Olivier's life and work: Douglas Fairbanks with his Order of Merit, Michael Caine carrying his Oscar, Maggie Smith with the model of Chichester Festival Theatre, Paul Scofield with the silver model of the Royal National Theatre, Derek Jacobi bearing the crown worn by Olivier in the film of *Richard III*, Jean Simmons carrying the film script for *Hamlet*, Ian McKellen with the laurel-wreath used in *Coriolanus* and Dorothy Tutin with the

crown used in the televised *King Lear*; and finally Frank Finlay, Iago
to Olivier's Othello, carrying the sword presented to Olivier by John
Gielgud and once owned by Edmund Kean. Each is placed before
the high altar, within a stone's throw of the tomb of Henry V
and the grave of Lady Anne, queen to Richard III.

I speak in my introductory bidding of the unique and awesome
talent God gave Olivier, of how for sixty years he astonished, moved
and teased his public, interpreting human nature at its noblest, its
most comic and its most pitiable. Albert Finney reads from Ecclesi-
astes and John Mills from Corinthians, and the choir sing Psalm
150 and Vaughan Williams' lovely 'Valiant for Truth' from *The
Pilgrim's Progress*. Peggy Ashcroft reads an extract from Milton's
Lycidas, and Gielgud reads John Donne's 'Death be not proud'; and
then, with tears in his eyes, unexpectedly adds those touching
words from *Hamlet* which end, 'The readiness is all'. Alec Guinness
pays tribute in a beautifully judged address, quoting Coleridge's
words about Edmund Kean: 'To see him act is like reading Shakespeare by flashes of lightning'; of how Olivier's 'sense of the mystery
of things never left him'; of his war-time service in the Fleet Air
Arm ('He did, I believe, quite a bit of damage, but not to the
enemy'); and he too ends with words from *Hamlet*:

Good night, sweet prince,
And flights of angels sing thee to thy rest.

The 'Agincourt Song' (Walton again) is played on the organ, and
Olivier's own voice fills the Abbey with the Crispin speech from
Henry V; then – following the prayers – the choristers sing the
haunting dirge from *Cymbeline*: 'Fear no more the heat o' the sun'.

After the blessing, I read Henry V's words after the Agincourt
victory:

Do we all holy rites:
Let there be sung *Non nobis* and *Te Deum*
The dead with charity enclos'd in clay.
And then to Calais; and to England then;
Where ne'er from France arriv'd more happy men.

And from the organ loft the choir fills the Abbey with the rich Christian affirmation of Walton's *Coronation Te Deum*.

There was huge press coverage, by and large sympathetic, even admiring. A few thought it was over the top, but then so was Olivier from time to time, stylishly so, and it was a memorial service for this particular actor, and therefore one that needed to have both an internal integrity and keep faith with the sort of man he was. It also had to be an act of worship that met the needs of those who came (in the words of my bidding) 'to remember him before God with gratitude, to ask of God forgiveness for his faults, and to celebrate the gifts which have enhanced all our lives'. Almost without exception they were those whose life is in the theatre, many of whom might not have wished to define too closely just what they believed or did not believe, but who nevertheless felt a powerful need for some sense of completion, for the drawing of a line under a great actor's life with a real sense of occasion in this unique place. We need rituals and commemorations, not least for our own sake. But they can raise all sorts of questions which also relate to integrity. That integrity has to do partly with the need to be faithful to the person who has died, guarding (as it were) *their* integrity; but it also has to do with the church's integrity as the guardian of a distinctive understanding of each human life in the light of Gospel truths, and her appropriate role at a time of common grief. When, for example, Philip Larkin's memorial service took place in the Abbey in 1985, Dean Edward Carpenter said in his bidding:

We give thanks for his intellectual integrity which would not allow him to accept the consolations of faith which he could not share and which would have delivered him from a fear of dying by which all his life he was haunted.

That was well said. Such questions of integrity are of particular concern to a church which is so exposed and in the public eye, but they are no less relevant to other more modest churches, for they are about people's needs and expectations and the fine line between discretion and excess. (Princess Diana's funeral was the classic example of having to resolve this quandary, though that was no longer my responsibility, and as a member of the congregation at that extraordinary service I felt a mixture of pride and admiration at how successfully the Abbey had held the ring in the face of so many public and conflicting interests and emotions.)

The newly produced Church of England Lectionary and Collects, concerned to update the phrase about withstanding **'the temptations of the world, the flesh and the devil'**, have given us an alternative collect for this Sunday. It asks God instead to

grant to all those who are admitted into the fellowship of Christ's religion, that they may reject those things that are contrary to their profession, and follow all such things as are agreeable to the same . . .

which is saying much the same thing. There is an ambiguity in the New Testament about the words 'world' and 'flesh'. When he contrasts 'flesh' and 'spirit', St Paul is not falling into some kind of dualism, saying that one is weak and sinful and the other good. Jesus came 'in the flesh'. Human beings are a complex entity and all of a piece. What Paul is saying is that to live 'according to the flesh' means to live solely by the world's standards, to live with our whole personality wrongly directed; to live as if Christ had not come, the Holy Spirit had not been given. In that best of classics on the life of the spirit, *Centuries*, Thomas Traherne writes of how quickly we are tarnished, losing our childhood innocence as we learn 'the dirty devices of this world'; and for St John (who tends to see things in black and white) 'the world' means human society alienated from God and blind to his presence. Christians are to be 'in the world but not of it', believing that God was revealed in Jesus Christ 'because he so loved the *world*' and longs to restore it to its true God-centred life; their role to affirm the values of the Kingdom which Jesus disclosed, that state of being in which God's sovereignty is acknowledged. His is a vision of a world in which people are more concerned with giving than with having, with sharing than with possessing, with serving than with being served; where each is valued for what he or she *is* rather than what they *have*; where the narrow loyalties of class or race or tradition or party are of less weight than the solidarity of the human race created in God's likeness; and where in areas of conflict and violence forgiveness and reconciliation have been proved to be the most powerful of all weapons.

So it may be that we need not only to challenge the subtle attraction of some of the world's values but sometimes turn them on their head. And I used to wonder what were the implications of the need to be 'in the world but not of it' for the members of an established church, and in particular for one that is also perceived to be at the heart of what is loosely called 'the Establishment'.

Two things help to make the Abbey unique. The first is that it embraces the ancient parish church of St Margaret's, Westminster, which is not in fact a separate parish but an integral part of the Abbey. St Margaret's is the church intimately associated with Parliament, the place, for example, where the service for MPs at the start of a new Parliament and almost all Parliamentary memorial services take place. The second is that, while the Abbey is looked to throughout the world as the national church, the historic site for coronations, royal weddings and funerals, and services to mark momentous state occasions, it is one of those independent churches known rather oddly as 'royal peculiars'. It comes directly under its Visitor, the Queen, and is answerable to no bishop or archbishop. Thus it is both bound and free: locked (to some extent) into its expected role and stamped by its history, but almost uniquely free in how it chooses to conduct its affairs and respond to requests of refreshingly diverse kinds.

For example: I think of a day of prayer for the homeless just before Christmas 1992, which we organised with the Churches' National Housing Coalition, which exists to express united Christian concern about the poverty and desperation caused by the lack of affordable housing, the poverty so painfully visible on the streets of all our cities; to keep the need for decent homes high on the public agenda; and to urge Government to tackle the question of homelessness as a priority and with a conviction that it has often lacked. Two days later, before a Lobby of Parliament, a thousand people filled the nave for a strong, unconventional service at which the Archbishop of Canterbury called for 'a moral crusade to rid society of the evil of homelessness', and church leaders of many traditions, together with African drummers, took part in the liturgy. This was not an attack on the Tory administration: it was an expression of a concern for social justice by Christians of all political persuasions who well understood the complexity of the problem but were united in their belief that societies are judged on the value they place on their most marginalised members.

I think, too, of the moving service we had held in the quire in the previous year for the 6th International Conference for People with HIV/AIDS, with music and dance and poetry, and the informal unfolding of inscribed quilts, while Ian McKellen and Dorothy Tutin read the names of those who had died from AIDS, in the presence of hundreds of people from all over the world, many of whom were very sick and others of whom were caring for them. Rarely has an act of worship in the Abbey so clearly recognised and met an expressed need, yet what gave it a more potent significance was that all who came were being welcomed into this 'Establishment' church which only hours before had witnessed a totally contrasting event: a rehearsal for the annual Battle of Britain Service to be held on the following day, with its ceremonial, its trumpets, its marching feet.

It is, of course, the scope of the demands made on the Abbey that makes it so challenging: 520 special services, I reckoned, in ten years (325 in the Abbey, 195 in St Margaret's), roughly one each week in addition to the nineteen hundred annual daily and Sunday services: for the 'specials' are always undergirded by the daily rhythm of prayer and offices and sacrament. I pluck a handful of diary entries from a crowded decade almost at random, to illustrate something of their variety.

27 June 1988

Service of Thanksgiving for Bishop Michael Ramsey. So many loved him for his goodness, his prayerfulness, his often awkward but wise and perceptive presence. Children, students and former chaplains process with his pectoral cross, the ring given him by the Pope, his Canterbury cap, a copy of his book *Canterbury Pilgrim*, his stole, his wooden pastoral staff. There are brief readings from a dozen of his books, and hymns and prayers which he and I had discussed before he died. In his address Professor Owen Chadwick says: 'Children thought he was the nearest thing to God: Michael Ramsey thought they were. There are those in this Abbey who think both were right.'

21 April 1989

A terrible earthquake in Armenia has killed many thousands. There is a large community of Armenians in London and they come tonight to Evensong sung by the choir, followed by an address by Archbishop Runcie. What follows is deeply touching. The Armenian bishop leads us in prayer, and the Armenian choir then sing the haunting Orthodox Office of the Dead. Many are in tears.

24 January 1991

The Gulf War began a week ago. There are virtually no American tourists and greatly reduced numbers all round. The whole mood of the Abbey has changed. As a Chapter we are divided in our view of the morality of the war, but not in our belief that the Abbey must be neutral ground where all may come and sit and pray. Many do so. We spotlight the Unknown Warrior's Grave and light candles with appropriate prayer-cards before all the altars. Tonight there is an ecumenical *Songs of Praise* in the nave, televised live by the BBC. Intercessions are led by the three service chaplains, a black bishop from the Assembly of God and a member of the Society of Friends. The most moving moment is when a senior Muslim, Dr Zaki Badawi, and the Jewish Rabbi, Hugo Gryn, read alternate verses of the 23rd Psalm, and at the end of it clasp hands in a symbolic act of friendship. Two days ago the Iraqis launched Scud missiles against Tel Aviv.

4 May 1991

A service for the centenary of the British Deaf Association. The Abbey is full to overflowing with the profoundly deaf. Everywhere there are individuals translating the service into sign language. What is striking is the great variety of style: near me a young woman signs with such expressiveness and grace that it gives new meaning to 'the word made flesh'. A dozen totally deaf children stand on a rostrum in the middle of the choir and sing

> Let there be peace on earth and let it begin with me,
> Let me walk with my neighbour in perfect harmony.

They sign it, making what noise they can, and are surrounded by our boy choristers who sing with them. The integration of able and disabled singing those words is especially poignant.

18 November 1991

Yesterday at Morning Prayer the Old Testament lesson from Proverbs contained the words: 'Like cold water to the throat that is faint with thirst is good news from a distant land.' A few hours later comes

36

the news that the hostage Terry Waite has been released after five years. At once we draw up a service of thanksgiving for tonight and fax details to the press and the BBC. As a result 750 people come as the Abbey bells ring out, together with the Archbishop of Canterbury, the Lord Chancellor and the Speaker of the House of Commons, and we thank God both for Terry's safe return home, and also for the spirit of human endurance, that unembittered and quiet strength that was evident three months ago in John McCarthy and now in Terry Waite, which ought to rekindle our confidence in the power of the human spirit to resist evil and draw out of it something that is creative and good.

23 October 1992

As we planned the service to mark the 50th anniversary of that turning-point in the War, the Battle of El Alamein, all of us were determined that it should not be a triumphalist occasion, but a real remembering of those who sacrificed their lives, and a rededication to work for peace and justice in the new Europe. The Queen and the Prince and Princess of Wales are present and it is televised. The first part is in the nave, centred on the Grave of the Unknown Warrior. Godfrey Talbot, BBC War Correspondent at El Alamein, reads one of his scripts broadcast from the battlefield. Children from Britain, the Commonwealth, Germany, Italy and Egypt follow standard-bearers through the Abbey and place bouquets of flowers on the high altar. Prayers are said by German and Italian chaplains, lessons read by the respective sons of the opposing generals, Viscount Montgomery and Dr Manfred Rommel. I find it so strange, remembering how as a schoolboy I stuck flags in the map of North Africa as that desert campaign unfolded, and how a proudly chirpy Monty came to my school in 1943 to lecture us on how he won the battle of El Alamein, that Montgomery and Rommel are drinking coffee together in the Deanery drawing-room.

21 December 1994

It is exactly five years since the Pan Am jet exploded over Lockerbie at 7.03 p.m. Tonight, as Big Ben strikes seven, most of the relatives and friends of those who died are gathered in the nave. Dr Jim Swire, who lost his daughter, has made a massive structure containing 272 candles and these are lit as the names are read out. The father of one young victim gives a short address on the need to overcome evil with good. The candles have been mounted on a gently-sloping frame with mirrors at both ends. This means that, placed as it is before the nave altar, the lit candles are reflected over and over again until it looks like a small stairway to heaven.

One night I took the then Religious Affairs Correspondent for the BBC, Mike Wooldridge, around the Abbey. A few days later he was back for a special Sunday evening One World Week service that focused on refugees and asylum-seekers. The next day he wrote in a letter:

The service was a sobering event, particularly because Colin Semper announced during the course of it the death of a Nigerian earlier in the day while police and immigration officers were at his flat. Being in the Abbey at that moment had echoes of being in Johannesburg Cathedral for campaigning services in the eighties. The topicality of the event contrasted so greatly with the richness of the history you described for me on the previous Thursday evening. And I remember how moving I had found it to listen to extracts from the ANC service (which the Abbey arranged) on the night Mandela was released. That the Abbey can make you feel awed, intimate, celebratory and angry at different times is testimony to its being so much more than walls and a roof.[1]

I always believed that the Abbey's role, like the Church's role, is to be loyal to its heritage but not encumbered by it. In short, to distinguish its inheritance from its tradition. The former is what we inherit from the past, what the dead have chosen to leave to the living: the family silver or the family portraits; in the Abbey's case, a wonder of stone and wood and glass and an over-abundance of tombs and memorials. We're stuck with them, willy-nilly. But our *tradition* – the church's living tradition – is subtly different. For that is not simply what we, the living, inherit from the past. It is what we value and believe to be worth preserving because it still speaks to us and is still relevant. That is the test we have to apply to the monarchy, or the laws by which we are governed, or the kind of society we want to create, and it is no less true of the church. We have to discern what realities are permanently true and of value and communicate them in language that links with life as most people experience it, with all its heartbreak and delight and mystery. No doubt an annual service that looks to the past, like that to commemorate those who died in the Battle of Britain, while important for my and my parents' generation, will only survive as long as there are some alive who fought in it or who remember it; we no longer observe the Battles of Agincourt or Waterloo. Yet it will always be the church's task to be a living reminder both of the unchanging nature of the Christ-like God, and also of what makes us human: of enduring truths like an abiding concern for justice, or compassionate support for the poor, the oppressed, the sick and the afflicted.

The potential conflict between faithfulness to the Gospel and what the state expected of the Abbey as a church that was both established and 'Establishment', occasions that would force us to decide whether we should '**reject those things that are contrary to (our) profession**' because they were 'of the world', seemed to be minimal. And that sometimes bothered me. I remember standing with my colleagues at the west door, waiting to welcome more than one Head of State, knowing that in their country human rights were abused, with demonstrators shouting behind the police barriers as they arrived, and wondering: 'Is it our corporate duty to combine the usual smiling welcome with the usual friendly tour – or can I risk saying things which will outrage the officials at the Foreign and Commonwealth Office who are hoping for successful trade talks or a new arms deal, or

whatever?' I am not proud of the fact that, perhaps inevitably, I compromised, easing my conscience by adding a
prayer (after the standard prayer for peace) for justice and
the recognition of human rights – for somehow the fact that
it was addressed to God rather than the dictator by my side
weakened its impact.

Far subtler questions lurked around one of our most public
and publicised activities: the services that had to be devised
for great occasions, or for distinctive ones like the ones I
have quoted above. Some of these were memorial services
for one who had 'done the state some service'. It was not
simply, as with Olivier's thanksgiving service, a matter of
discerning the fine line between discretion and excess. It
was once again a question of integrity: the readiness to hear
what those closest to the event, or to the dead person, felt
was appropriate, and then keeping faith with their need and
desire and with Christian belief and custom. Often those
who met with us to plan such a service came with a limited
knowledge of resources or of the possibilities open to them,
but a clear expectation of what they wanted. And it was not
at all surprising that familiar language and well-tested
hymns and readings met people's expectations and needs
most effectively, especially at times of grief. For example, at
the service of thanksgiving for the life of Bobby Moore,
at which – as so often – a majority were not church-goers,
we included the most conventionally familiar 'top ten'
(Crimond, Bunyan's 'To be a pilgrim', 'Abide with me', 'Jerusalem', St Paul on love, and 'O for the wings of a dove!'),
and it was a service notable for a contained stillness and
sense of completion and (afterwards) gratitude. (The unfam-
iliar element was Jimmy Tarbuck's address. 'In terms of
nerves, this is for me, Dean, what top billing at the London
Palladium would be for you.') But if the familiar properly
formed at least the basis for such events we could usually
build on the well-known structure more unpredictable
pieces – as the Organist and Master of Choristers, Martin

Neary, did so imaginatively with his suggestion of John Tavener's *Athene* at the end of Princess Diana's funeral.

There was one annual occasion that in the light of the collect's request that we may **'follow you, the only God; through Jesus Christ our Lord'** needed a firm corporate decision: the multi-Faith Observance held in the presence of the Queen ('Defender of the Faith') on Commonwealth Day. After a somewhat chequered initial history it has taken place at the Abbey for twenty years. Colourful and cosmopolitan, representatives of all 50 Commonwealth nations parade in national costume with their flags. A West Indian steel band plays before and after the Observance. Leaders of all the world's great faiths (representing not only the Commonwealth but our highly diverse, pluralist society) read from their scriptures, and all affirm five shared beliefs: respect for the natural world, the worth of each person, the need to work for justice, peace and reconciliation, the supremacy of love and our membership of one human family.

Although the Observance is attended by leaders of all Christian traditions, there was explicit and noisy criticism by a faction of the Church and a protest was sent to the Queen. Much was made by our critics of Jesus' words: 'No one comes to the Father except by me'.[2] Yet that text relates specifically to the fatherhood of God: it is not simply a question of coming 'to God' but of coming 'to the Father'. There is but one God, 'in whom we live and move and have our being', and when we worship we stand before the mystery of that deep and eternal Reality to whom we give different names. From Jews we learn of his faithfulness; from Muslims of his sovereignty and mercy; from the wonders of the natural world a realisation of his mystery and power. Christians speak of something more intimate: of his *fatherhood*, for only in Jesus can we begin to experience the truth of God as Father. The presence of those from the Commonwealth of other faiths, each person praying to God as that

41

faith conceives him to be, did nothing to compromise our belief that in Jesus Christ we see the ultimate expression of God's nature, for that belief does not deny the truth of other revelations of God, nor our hope that in Christ all may ultimately find their fulfilment. As was strongly spelled out and understood, it is to the incarnational God that the Abbey has borne witness throughout its history, and it always will.

In considering **'the temptations of the world, the flesh and the devil'**, the need to **'reject those things that are contrary to [our Christian] profession, and follow all such things as are agreeable to the same'**, I have chosen to highlight a potential conflict between what the Gospel demands and what the world (especially the State) may require. I want to end this chapter on a much more personal note: the question of role-playing. For that goes to the heart of our human/Christian dilemma, and nowhere is it more evident than in the life of a priest. Playing a role can be both constructive and destructive. Take clergy: it can seem that they (perhaps like therapists) are never quite free of their role, by which I mean that it is very hard for people not to set them apart or think of them as 'different'. I am not thinking of the many who dismiss them as redundant or deluded, dinosaur figures from a past, more credible age; I mean those who relate to them as members of their congregations. For priests can never be quite free of their professionalism. They hear a lot of secrets, listening for hours to those who are vulnerable and who have dared to confide in a counsellor in absolute trust and often at some cost; and at the end of the day it is the priest's professional role that must guarantee this and make it possible. A certain recognised 'apartness'. And this necessary role is something a priest accepts and takes on, something partly defined by the valid expectations and needs of others.

But if a priest is chiefly pastor, his or her other traditional role is to be the leader of worship, to be at the sharp end during services, guiding and shaping the words and the liturgy from altar, stall and pulpit. It is a different sort of role, and means you can never be as wholly relaxed or receptive in church as others can; that's part of the cost of ministry. Where things go wrong, sometimes disastrously so, is where the priest *becomes* the role, where there is nothing left that is not the role. A priest I once knew, when meeting a stranger, never said, 'I am Rupert Bear', but always, 'I am the Archdeacon of X.' And Donald Nicholl once described being at a meeting where they sat in a group and had to introduce themselves, and they all did so in terms of their jobs or professions. 'When it came to my turn,' he said, 'all I wanted to say was: "My name is Donald, and I am a unique manifestation of God".' For if you identify solely with your role it can begin to destroy your humanity, and you may even become a dehumanising force within the community. A Samson whose hair has been shorn, and you know it not. Processing round the Abbey in a cope, or sitting as we did in a scarlet cassock and black gown in Chapter (part of the heritage, you understand), as Dean, Sub-Dean, Canon Treasurer, and so on, it was all too easy to become the role.

Gerard Hughes writes of how, after many years of running the tertianship in a Jesuit seminary, he realised

that I was not primarily a priest or a Jesuit. Primarily I am a human being and only remain priest and Jesuit because for me, with my temperament, upbringing and inclination, this seems a good way of being human.[3]

One day I was having lunch in our small Choir School in order to meet the new boys. One eight-year-old was sitting on my right, and I spent a long while trying unsuccessfully to get him to talk. He was totally monosyllabic – yet as he ate he never took his eyes off me. It was a very cool, if silent, assessment. Finally, just before we rose to say grace, he said: 'So, *basically* you're the Dean of Westminster.' Well, of course for him role and person were one and the same, but *basically* I was – well, what was I? The Dean? No: basically I was me. Me as I have always been; me, in essence, as I always shall be: nobody's role-model and nobody's clone. But, much of the time, playing a role of a different sort. As we all do. The role we play in seeking (often quite unconsciously) to conform to certain stereotypes of male or female, husband or wife, parent or child; but – more to the point – conforming to the model of what the world expects of us, conforming to prevailing values and shifting ideas. Perhaps that's inevitable, part of what it means to be human.

Yet isn't that the point? For 'being human' doesn't have to be constricting: it can be liberating. What it means to be human has been redefined by so many whose bodies or memorials lie in the Abbey: Spenser and Shakespeare, Keats and Milton and Wordsworth, Hardy and Dickens, Handel and Henry Purcell. They are among those who explored the mystery of what it means to be human in compelling words and music. Here lie the bones of Darwin, Isaac Newton, Faraday, Rutherford and Kelvin. They are among those who combined a probing intellect with a leap of intuitive imagination and unlocked some of the secrets of the natural world. Here are Gladstone and Pitt, Wilberforce and Shaftesbury, Churchill and Attlee and Ernest Bevin. They are among those who sought to build a common life based on equity, freedom and justice.

But there is a much more complete definition of what a person is and could be. As I have said, it was not just God who was being redefined in Jesus Christ: it was *us*. ('I have come that they may have life, and may have it in all its fullness'.[4]) And 'to be admitted into the fellowship of Christ's religion' is to change your understanding of what human is. What human can become if and when we turn and open ourselves to the life-changing power of the Father's love. It is not 'the great and the good' in the worldly sense who reveal the true power and potential of a human life:

we glimpse it, rather, in those who attract us by some aspect of Christ-likeness, acknowledged or unacknowledged. In some it may take the form of a trusting stillness, an integrity, a kind of transparency; in others, a passionate concern for justice or a generosity of spirit. Or compassion. Or courage in the face of adversity. Or the readiness to forgive, whatever the cost. Or, perhaps, what Stendhal called the quality of the 'happy few'.

The happy few . . . are those who remain emotionally alive, who never compromise, who never succumb to cynicism or the routine of the second-hand. The happy few are not necessarily happy. But they are never corrupted and seldom bored. The happy few possess what Baudelaire calls 'impeccable *naïveté*', the ability to see the world always afresh, either in its tragedy or its hope.[5]

Where we catch a glimpse of how we might be, we want it.

Yet human also means fragile, and communities are delicate structures, made up as they are of fragile people. The surprising thing is not that they often fail, not that there are occasional crises or scandals, rows or misunderstandings, but that they so often succeed. The sad thing is that we live at a time when something like three-quarters of any mention of God, Christianity or religion in the media is either negative or contemptuous and, because Christian bodies are perceived to be claiming to be better than others, they are all the more vigorously condemned when they fail. The truth, of course, is that we are claiming no such thing: in fact, the complete opposite. We are acknowledging daily that we are sinners who need to be – and will be – endlessly forgiven, and who know what it means to be reconciled and restored. No one knew this more painfully than that model of a parish priest George Herbert:

> Profaneness in my head,
> Defects and darkness in my breast,

A noise of passions ringing me for dead
Unto a place where is no rest.

His consolation lies in the fixed mark of God's forgiveness,
and (more mysteriously) in St Paul's conviction that 'The
life I now live is not my life, but the life which Christ lives
in me',[6] which in Herbert becomes:

Christ is my only head,
My alone only heart and breast,
My only music, striking me even dead,
That to the old man I may rest,
And be in him new drest.[7]

Sin is our refusal to become who we truly are. In those
moments when I kneel before God in penitence, or join
with others in confession, sometimes I am aware of specific
faults: unloving words, thoughtless conduct, selfish actions.
I am aware of not caring enough. But chiefly I am aware of
a much more subtle temptation: to settle for less than I
might be. To choose the lesser good. To lack curiosity and
wonder. To miss the mark because my sights are fixed too
low. Not to perceive that I am 'fearfully and wonderfully
made' in God's image. And when I ask God to forgive me, I
do so because, in settling for less than I am created to be,
I know not what I do.

Lord God Almighty,
grant your people grace
to withstand the temptations
of the world, the flesh, and the devil,
of conforming to worldly standards and values,
of settling for less than you made us to be,
and with pure hearts and minds
to follow you, the only God;
through Jesus Christ our Lord.

LENT III
St Edward's Shrine

On suffering, loneliness and vulnerability

Almighty God,
whose most dear Son went not up to joy
** but first he suffered pain,**
and entered not into glory before he was crucified:
mercifully grant that we, walking in the way of the cross,
may find it none other than the way of life and peace;
through Jesus Christ our Lord.

As the light and the seasons change, so does the appearance and feel of the Abbey. I came to know and love it in every mood, but never did it seem more enchanted than late on Christmas Eve. By 9.30 everything had been prepared for the Midnight Mass, when people would be packed into every corner, and for an hour the building was empty and totally silent, the hundreds of tiny lights on the tall Christmas tree at one end of the nave and the spotlights on the wooden Oberammergau figures of the crib at the other the only source of light, so that the tall columns climbed into darkness and the vaulted roof was full of shadows. I would walk very slowly from the west door, through the nave and quire, up the steps to the sanctuary and through the narrow door in the Victorian reredos to the most hallowed part of the Abbey: the Chapel of St Edward the Confessor. And kneeling before his shrine, in which his body still rests, I would, in that strangely potent stillness, feel something of the wonder of the Word made flesh, celebrated in this space for nearly a thousand years.

It was 13 October 1269, St Edward's Day, when the Confessor's body was finally carried to the dazzling new tomb erected for him by Henry III. Contemporary accounts of Edward's life are more hagiography than history. He seems to have been the usual human mix: in his case piety (spending days together at Mass and at his devotions), a real concern for the poor and the infirm, a noted gentleness and austerity, but also sudden explosions of anger and a love for flying his hawks and hunting with hounds. It was he who decided to turn the small Benedictine monastery at Westminster into a magnificent Romanesque church, and to build an adjacent palace and court. He just saw the Abbey's completion on Holy Innocents' Day, 1065, dying eight days later. His burial in the Abbey, and his canonisation a century later, ensured that the Abbey became the coronation church of the kings and queens of England. Edward's body was moved to its first shrine on 13 October 1163, in the presence of Henry II and Archbishop Thomas Becket, and it became 'one of the sights of medieval England',[1] attracting a flood of pilgrims, many of whom came to pray for healing at the tomb of one with a reputation for holiness and a growing reputation for the miraculous. When Henry III pulled down Edward's Abbey in the thirteenth century, it was in order to pay Edward even greater honour by constructing the present Gothic Abbey with the saint's shrine at its centre. The new shrine he created cost £5000 (the equivalent today of £1.8 million),

for the kynge grievid that the relics of saint Edward were poorly enshrined ... and resolved that so great a luminary should not be buried, but should be placed high as on a candlestick to enlighten the church.[2]

The base (which alone survives the desecration of later ages, and the turbulence of the Reformation, when it ceased to be an object of reverence and became a superstitious relic of a papal past) is of Purbeck marble, decorated with mosaic. Above it was the Confessor's coffin encased in a shrine of pure gold, decorated with 11 small golden images of kings and saints; the whole embedded with jewels. It stood proud on four steps, gleaming in the dark building and drawing the eye; and in the lower part were recesses in which sick persons knelt. As I did still on Christmas Eve.

A constant Lenten theme, spelled out in collects and readings, is that of Christ's suffering and vulnerability. Truths which pierce to the very heart of that redefinition of God which is what Christian belief is about. A God who does not give simple answers to Job in his anguish, for Job must learn that there are absolute limits to the extent of human understanding; a God who, by his awesome gift of human freedom, cannot prevent the cancer cell or the Holocaust; a God who, but for one thing, would seem an uncaring tyrant. But it is that one thing that changes everything: the claim that God does not give answers. There are no answers. Instead, he gives himself. The most perceptive of the Old Testament writers had written of a God who shares his people's joys and sufferings. Hosea pictures his relationship with his people in terms of one who says: 'I took them in my arms . . . I secured them with reins and led them with bonds of love . . . I lifted them like a little child to my cheek, (and) bent down to feed them.'[3]

But it was inspired guesswork: for how can we know that the unimaginable God suffers and has compassion – any more than (to use Isaac Bashevis Singer's analogy) a slow-worm crawling inside a copy of *War and Peace* can be a critic of Tolstoy? What Christians claim is that he can and does, that in Jesus, rather than providing answers, he enters into the questions – and in so doing transforms them. Enters into them in the only terms we can recognise and understand, in terms of one man's birth, life and painful death. Jesus comes to be the love of God in our midst. That, and nothing less than that, is what every church exists to proclaim, that in the words of Dietrich Bonhoeffer, 'Only a suffering God can help', or in words of John Austin Baker, 'The crucified Jesus is the only accurate picture of God the world has ever seen'. And so our most painful human wounds are most intimately connected to the sufferings of God himself, for in Christ he too knows (though this is where human language falters and ultimately fails) what it is to live, to know pain at its potentially most destructive, to face desolation and to die. **'He went not up to joy but first he suffered pain.'**

In his life Jesus sought out the sick and the sinful, the damaged and those who were held in contempt, and in his death he was numbered with transgressors and crucified between thieves, for each is valued and all lie within the embrace of the suffering God. What the gospels tell is of one who comes alongside us and identifies, not with the self-righteous, but with those who are the outcasts of society, thereby giving them a sense of their dignity. By supporting them Jesus sets them free to discover their worth in his eyes and therefore in God's sight too. Grace Jantzen has written of how in Psalm 22, which was on the lips of Jesus on the cross, and

which the church has regularly taken as descriptive of Christ, one of the qualities calling forth awe is his readiness to be alongside a sufferer:

> For he has not despised or abhorred the affliction of the
>   afflicted;
> and he has not hid his face from him,
> but has heard, when he cried to him.[4]

This is what the incarnation means: God's solidarity with humankind in all our need and vulnerability. And we are judged on how well we recognise both each other's vulnerability and that human need to be affirmed and encouraged wherever it may surface. Sometimes the obligation is over-whelming in its impact upon us – diseased and starving children in Africa or Iraq have equal claim on our com-passion – but there are other times when the church seems unaware that its voice should be heard, or reluctant to come alongside those who (for whatever reason) are afflicted and need support. Ten years ago that appeared to be the case with those affected by the HIV/AIDS virus, and I was con-vinced that the Abbey must give a lead in making more people aware of the church's role as a non-judgemental, caring body in the face of human suffering, however that suffering has come about.

We did so in three ways. I have spoken of the International AIDS Day Service, after which the organisers wrote of how the delegates from many nations 'were impressed that this site of British tradition and establishment was so willing to welcome people with HIV and AIDS. Once again the HIV community has cause to be grateful to the Dean and Chapter for their solidarity with us'; we also hosted special services for World AIDS Day and for the London Lighthouse to mark its tenth anniversary, when commemorative quilts, each a patchwork of names of those who had died, were spread all over the floor of the nave and sanctuary. I also invited, over a period of six years, actors of the calibre of Alec Guinness and Judi Dench, Paul Scofield, Ian McKellen and Peggy Ashcroft (her last engagement before she died) to come once a month to Richard II's fourteenth-century Jerusalem Chamber and read their own choice of poetry or prose before an audience of 50 people who had paid £10 for a ticket and a glass of wine. All the money went to AIDS charities, which benefited to the tune of £16,000.[5] But the chief way in which we tried to 'show solidarity' was by arranging quar-terly supper parties in the Jerusalem Chamber for those affected by the virus or living with it.

7 October 1996

For me, the last of the supper parties which I began seven years ago. Each evening has taken the same form. We invite some 40 people and during the first hour we meet each other and share in a buffet; then we sit in a wide circle around the room. I tell them a little of its history: of how Henry IV died here in 1413; of how Elizabeth Woodville, queen to Edward IV, had sought sanctuary here with her younger son, Richard, when the future Richard III had imprisoned his brother, Edward, in the Tower; of how a large part of the 1611 King James version of the Bible had been translated here by a committee of scholars presided over by Dean Lancelot Andrewes. Then each person in the circle, if they wish, speaks briefly of who they are and why they have come. Many are sick, a few with not long to live; tonight there are parents of a young man who has died, partners and carers, plus a handful of those working full-time as doctors, nurses or chaplains in AIDS wards or hospices. As always, some are Christians, many are not; and time and again the latter have said (as they do tonight) how surprised and glad they are to have been included.

But tonight there is one difference. For I have invited Diana, Princess of Wales, to come, and she does so, unaccompanied and without my warning those present. She arrives at eight, and I witness what so many have spoken of – her immediate and instinctive knowledge of what to do: whom to touch, whose hand to hold, and what to say. After half an hour we go into the Abbey for a relaxed tour of the empty, awesome building, ending in St Faith's Chapel for some moments of stillness and the briefest of night prayers and a blessing. (Once a Franciscan led a short, memorable meditation on the Isenheim crucifix, that extraordinary painting from the time when the Black Death was sweeping through Europe, in which Christ's scourged body is covered with a mass of boils and black spots.) I never fail to be moved by how affected they are by the atmosphere in this historic, holy and storied space. Although I use words with which to tell its story, it is invariably the space that speaks. And afterwards I always feel: 'This is as close as we get to the heart of what we are *for*.'

There were those who criticised this ministry, usually on one of two grounds. Was it right to place so great an emphasis on just one disease? What about other life-threatening illnesses where the numbers afflicted are greater, and the need for research is just as great? To which the answer was that to be effective you must be selective; you cannot spread your net too wide. And here was a peculiarly modern disease which was spreading through the world like wildfire and where the Church seemed muzzled in its response, often for reasons that formed the second ground of complaint. Many were infected with the virus through casual sex, and at that stage it seemed to be a disease largely affecting homosexuals (though by 1994 three-quarters of those worldwide who carried the AIDS virus did so as the result of heterosexual acts). Should not the Church be more judgemental than sympathetic? To which the strongest possible answer was the necessary distinction between affirming a principle and responding with care to anyone who is in need. By affirming sick individuals we were not denying our belief that the sexual act is properly the sign and seal of a long-term, loving commitment between two people. We were asserting something equally valid: that we have no right to judge others, nor to patronise or pity them. Instead we have the duty, in the presence of one who is suffering, hurt and anxious, to find a practical way of expressing that imaginative understanding to which we give the name of love.

I have learned so much from the AIDS community (if all those special individuals I have known will forgive such a clumsily generic term) about the meaning of that generous, self-giving love that is *agape*. Learned afresh that God is encountered in wounded people and communities, where human need is met by the unconditional response of doctors and nurses, partners, carers and befrienders. Even out of such pestilence come seeds of redemption, proving that there is something that is Godlike (which is to say Christ-like) in human beings to be recognised and affirmed. A Church which becomes inward-looking and exclusive, wanting to draw firm lines around its borders, either for credal or moral reasons, is unlikely to recognise the Christ-like in unexpected people and surprising places, for it does not yet understand the wisdom of the saying: 'When you approach another person, whatever their belief or lack of it, take off your shoes, for you are entering holy ground, and God has been there before you.'[6]

I wrote above that the suffering and vulnerability of Jesus is a persisting theme of the Lenten collects and readings. This week's collect speaks of us **'walking in the way of the cross'**. To be vulnerable is not a weakness: it is part of what it means to be human. Of course there are degrees of vulnerability. We are, most of us, very woundable creatures, and we may be wounded as a result of hurts suffered in childhood or later, wounds which may prove so traumatic that they seriously damage our ability to relate to others or to believe in God or in our own worth; but the vulnerability of Jesus is not that. Isaiah, in those strangely prophetic Servant Songs, speaks of the expected Messiah as one who 'will be wounded for our transgressions',[7] and it is that woundability, *that capacity to suffer on behalf of others* (which lies at the heart of love) that identifies him with us and us with him. If we lacked that vulnerability we should lack compassion. For the wounds come and no one wholly escapes them: in Blake's words:

> Man was made for Joy and Woe,
> And when that we rightly know,
> Through the world we safely go.
> Joy and Woe are woven fine,
> A clothing for the soul divine.[8]

Most of those who worship at the Abbey are strangers, their lives hidden. But over long years as a parish priest, privileged to share the intimacies of people's lives, I have sometimes marvelled as people come to kneel at the Communion rail at how many of them have known, or are bearing, some private grief or unhappiness. The daily toll of a parent with Alzheimer's. A disabled child. The pain of a broken marriage. The sudden loss of a job. The challenge of a long spell of sickness or a terminal illness. The anguish of an unrequited love. The numbness and the loneliness that follows the loss of a loved one. Those whom I have valued most on my own human journey have been those who speak or preach or write out of their own human experience, those who are ready at appropriate times, with reticence and hopefully without self-indulgence, to admit and share their own vulnerability. For my story is in its most resonant depths your story as well, and in telling you my story I shall in part be telling you your own, and this is because there is a larger story that unites us all. It is a story that alternates between the twin poles of loneliness and community. R. S. Thomas writes:

A pen appeared, and the god said:
'Write what it is to be
man.' And my hand hovered
long over the bare page,

until there, like footprints
of the lost traveller, letters
took shape on the page's
blankness, and I spelled out

the word 'lonely'. And my hand moved
to erase it; but the voices
of all those waiting at life's
window cried out loud: 'It is true.'[9]

There is a common story that unites us all. A story that speaks of the dark side of our planet: of the brokenness, failure, anger, guilt and pain, that are implicit in the costly business of loving and the unpredictability of human life. Any counseller knows that proper listening to another awakens all kinds of echoes in yourself, and that this recognition of what is so familiar to you marks the birth of that kind of empathy which is the beginning of healing. The loneliness has been met. A gulf has been bridged between one human being and another. Humanity, it has been said, is like an enormous spider's web, so that if you touch it anywhere, you set the whole thing trembling.

When I was first ordained, I remember my incumbent, who was a deeply spiritual, but also a deeply vulnerable man (and therefore a very good pastor) saying to me: 'When you are listening to someone's pain and need, remember to have one foot in the river as you stand beside them but always to keep one foot on the bank.' I knew what he meant, and I guess he was right. No counsellor will be of much help if both are floundering in deep waters, and you must be able to let go of people's problems when they have left you; but equally 'people are not problems to be solved, they are mysteries to be loved',[10] and they will only be attracted to you in the first place if they know from the sort of person you have revealed yourself to be that you are not afraid of sharing your own humanity.

Nothing I have ever done has surprised me more than the reaction to a small book I wrote as honestly as I could about the experience of a year's long, housebound illness (ME), and what it's like to be knocked flat in mid-journey; and the sort of questions one needs to ask if something good and creative is to be brought out of what is felt to be entirely negative and destructive. An elderly clerical friend was shocked by it: 'Do you enjoy undressing in public?' he asked. Yet the response took me by storm; after 11 years the book is still in print, and I've found it hard to cope with all the resulting letters; but what I now realise is that it is because telling my story has helped to authenticate other people's stories, not just (and this is the point) those whose time of darkness has taken the form of that much misunderstood illness, but other forms of illness or the pain of a marriage breakdown, or bereavement. Professionalism so often involves a holding back of large parts of oneself, an avoidance of the vulnerability that can only enhance our ability to be of help if we know, and can show others, how to use it creatively and redemptively.

Nor has any sermon I have ever preached brought a more interesting response than one I delivered from that daunting eyrie in St Paul's Cathedral for the annual service of the Sons of the Clergy about my father's suicide. It surprised me that so many of those present had relatives, friends, colleagues, who had taken their own lives and needed to hear this spoken of openly and within the context of the Christian faith. My father, whom I cannot remember, must have been the most vulnerable of men: the rector of a small country parish, one Saturday afternoon in May he wrote a note for my mother, climbed the tower of his church, removed the boarding from the belfry and threw himself down. He was found almost immediately by the gardener ('And Mary, supposing him to be the gardener . . .'[11]), asked for his shoelaces to be unloosed, and died. I was three. My mother was left homeless and virtually penniless. In those harsh days compassion seems to have been in short supply: a suicide was allowed no marked grave or memorial. 'I cannot conceive of a clergyman,' said the coroner at his inquest, 'desecrating holy ground, as Mr Mayne has done, unless his mind was very much deranged.' His ashes were scattered to the four winds, and nobody spoke of him again. What he was like, this wounded man whose genes I carry, or what deep unhappiness led him to take such a desperate action, I could only guess.

Until sixty years later. For sometimes life comes full circle in the most unpredictable of ways, and there is a kind of healing. A few old people in his parish remembered him and they and the rector felt there should be some memorial in the place he had served for five years. And so, three years ago, on my mother's ninety-fourth birthday, we returned with her grandchildren and great-grandchildren, and at the Eucharist a simple stone was placed in the chancel wall and I stood in my father's pulpit and after a lifetime tried to find words that echoed Hamlet's to his father's ghost: 'Rest, rest, perturbed spirit'; but much more, that spoke of that deepest of Christian insights: that even in the worst of events God is present and there are possibilities of redemption. That is part of the meaning of the cross: that good can be brought out of evil; that new life can emerge from an event that seems utterly final and devastating. With the local body of Christ that is now my father's parish I was saying to him: 'We shall never know *why* you did what you did, for that is known only to you and to God, but your desperate cry for help came out of so much unrecognised anguish of spirit that it demands not our judgement but our deep compassion.'

I also needed to say to my father that the rare photographs of him at which I have sometimes glanced merely catch my father's surface likeness: they tell us nothing of the secrets of the heart. His action has taught me that none of us can ever really understand the heart of another human being, and none of us dare pass judgement on anyone else's life or death. That is God's prerogative, for he alone perfectly understands, and his judgement is always more than matched by his mercy. Those who find life too painful or too complex to bear may have had the dice loaded against them from the start, and none of us know whether we would have survived if we had been in their place. What we do know is that the God who is our judge is also our saviour, and that in Jesus Christ all we need to know of God is once and for all defined. In the words of a friend who was eleven when his father committed suicide: 'I cannot tell how God was present in my father's death . . . but my faith and my prayer is that he was and that he continues to be present with him in ways beyond my guessing.'

The Gospel is about the reality of new life in Christ, about our healing, about 'the love that will not let me go'. Our eyes are to be fixed not 'on the things that are seen, but on the things that are unseen', for 'what is seen is transient; what is unseen is eternal . . . No wonder we do not lose heart.'[12] The God revealed by Jesus is not only our creator of whom the Psalmist writes,

> If I climb up to heaven, you are there;
> If I make the grave my bed, you are there also . . .[13]

but also our redeemer who, even as we turn to him in penitence, has forgiven us and welcomed us home. I do not believe my father needed me to tell him that. For I believe that when he fell to his death he was in the deepest sense caught and held in the everlasting arms of the one who is the merciful and loving Father of us all.

On that hot August day, as we gathered afterwards in the churchyard where he fell to his death, someone shyly approached my son and handed him a photocopy of the front page of a newspaper 'which may interest your father'. It was dated May 1932. It contained every detail of my father's act, of the coroner's inquest (and comments), of the simple funeral, things I had never known. And an old woman took me on one side and said: 'I was fifteen when he died. He was so popular in the village; and, you know, he was such a jolly man.' How little we reveal. How little we know.

Almighty God,
whose most dear Son went not up to joy
   but first he suffered pain,
and entered not into glory before he was crucified:

mercifully grant that we, walking in the way of the cross,
acknowledging our own wounded nature,
and acting with compassion towards those who suffer or are
    afflicted,
may find it none other than the way of life and peace;
through Jesus Christ our Lord.

5

MID-LENT BREATHER

Poets' Corner

On words and the Word

My most impressionable years were spent in south Devon during the War. I heard my first serious music and watched my first serious drama at Torquay Pavilion, a somewhat bizarre building in white marble, its copper roof crowned with two statues of Eros and an imposing Britannia. (Though not half as imposing as Olive Fox, wife of the summer concert party impresario, Clarkson Rose, who, as a hefty Britannia, draped in the Union Jack and clutching a trident, sang in the black days of 1940, 'There'll always be an England', one of my abiding memories of the War.) The Pavilion is still preserved, but now sadly down-graded into an assortment of boutiques. For wartime concerts the orchestra was somewhat reduced in size, both the conductor and the players elderly and short of puff, but classical music was a closed book to me and the afternoons on which I heard Myra Hess play Mozart, and Mark Hambourg play Brahms, were a revelation. Even more magical were the annual visits of the last of the great barn-storming actor-managers, Donald Wolfit, who would play Shylock, Macbeth and Lear in a single week. Wolfit, that flawed genius of an actor, with his own 'acting versions' of Shakespeare (he would bring the curtain down on *Hamlet* at the words 'and flights of angels sing thee to thy rest' in order to hold centre-stage to the end), and his somewhat dire supporting company, nevertheless opened up to this fifteen-year-old a new-found-land in which words took flight and sang.

Like many other only children I turned to books as a source of companionship. They fed my imagination and (along with films) were a means of escape from the unhappiness of those early wartime and immediately post-war school years and the loneliness of the holidays, spent with a bridge-playing grandmother in a seedy boarding-house, my mother having finally married again and gone to Africa. And then there arrived on the scene that one teacher, the one who (if you're lucky) is there at just the right moment and instils in you something of his or her own passion. In this case it was an old man, newly retired from his life's work, spending a kind of golden autumn teaching English at my school, and imparting his own enthusiasm for words and the poetry that had so enriched him. I can still recall the excitement of private tutorials with him as he prepared me for a scholarship exam (which I failed lamentably), and I guess his insights and Wolfit's passion began for me a lifetime's fascination with the mystery of words.

All of which lay behind the seductiveness of that part of the Abbey where so many dead authors lie around: Poets' Corner. The first writer to be buried in the southern transept of the Abbey was Geoffrey Chaucer, one-time Clerk of the Works at Westminster to Richard II. A plain grave on the floor marked his burial place in 1400 until, during that extraordinary outburst of literary genius in the Elizabethan age, in 1556 his bones were transferred to a fine tomb, and forty years later Edmund Spenser was buried near him. The fashion had begun. The pantheon of poets buried and memorialised in this space is both predictable and idiosyncratic, the considered – sometimes the capricious – choice of four centuries of deans, one of their few prerogatives. The Corner has grown organically, with no set rules of entry. Some of those who were always third-rate seem to have gained entry by paying for the privilege, though that poet laureate described by Sir Walter Scott as 'distinguished in everything but his poetry' failed to make it. But by and large this eclectic collection uniquely reflects the fashions of each age. Dean Stanley, one of the greatest of deans, wrote in 1876:

Successive Deans of Westminster ... have endeavoured to embrace, within the wide sympathy of their consecrated precincts, those whom a narrow and sectarian spirit might have excluded, but whom the precepts of their common Master, no less than the instincts of their common humanity, should have bid them welcome ... The godlike gift of genius was recognised – the baser earthly part was left to the merciful judgement of its Creator.[1]

On 1 April 1991 the *Times* Diary reported that the Abbey was planning to move memorials of lesser-known occupants to make way for 30 new claimants for entry. 'The names of David Niven, Beatrix Potter and John Lennon are expected to join Shakespeare in Poets' Corner', the diarist wrote, 'in the shake-up being planned by the Dean and Chapter'. Immediately the *Mail on Sunday* came on the line: did I not consider David Niven, though an attractive writer, a shade lightweight, someone to read on the beach? I asked the reporter if he had noticed the date. He hadn't.

In considering new names for memorialisation, my own criteria were whether a writer had made a major contribution to the literature of his or her nation; whether it seemed likely they would be remembered in a century's time – a hard one, that, fashion being so fickle – and whether in their lifetime they were so strongly disbelieving or anti-religious that to memorialise them in the Abbey would be an affront to their integrity. I agreed (with the backing of Chapter) to ten new memorials for writers in ten years, and had no doubts about any of them.[2]

13 June 1989
John Clare, rarest of men and best of nature poets, whose world centred on the tiny Northamptonshire parish of Helpston, and

whose poetry speaks simply and eloquently of parish joy and grief, the friend of Coleridge, Lamb and De Quincey, left school at the age of twelve. He was to spend 23 years in institutions, first in Matthew Allen's asylum in Epping Forest, then as a patient of Northampton General Lunatic Asylum. After his death word went round the village that a London surgeon had hired men to visit Helpston where they were to cut out Clare's brain to examine how a madman could write such poetry; 'Clare already knew where it came from: from clods of earth and from watching raindrops glittering on the backs of frogs.'[3] John Clare came in 1820 on his first tentative visit to London. He was taken to the theatre to see Kean and Macready, and he was brought to the Abbey to stand in wonder in Poets' Corner. Tonight the Poet Laureate, Ted Hughes, unveils a plaque in Westmoreland greenslate in his memory. Ronald Blythe speaks of how he celebrated the fields and woods and hedgerows of Helpston; Charles Causley reads his own poem 'Helpston', and two children from the village school bring wild flowers, tall grasses and poppies, picked this morning in the garden of his old cottage and conveyed here in ice-boxes with crushed aspirin to preserve them.

13 July 1993

The exact bicentenary of John Clare's birth. Ronald Blythe comes with what Clare would have known as a 'mid-summer cushion', wild flowers picked in a country garden and arranged in a great circle of thick moss: honeysuckle, deadnettle, bryony, clover, teazels, marguerites, St John's wort, hogweed, feverfew, yarrow, knapweed, ivy and heads of grass, wheat and barley. It lies tonight by his memorial stone.

10 October

To mark further the bicentenary, the actor Freddie Jones presents in the quire his one-man dramatised version of Clare's sad and moving life, raising £1500 for the National Schizophrenia Society.

14 February 1995

A hundred years ago tonight, on a bitter St Valentine's Day, *The Importance of Being Earnest* opened at the St James's Theatre. The Marquess of Queensbury, forbidden entry, left a bouquet of vegetables for Wilde at the stage door. Tonight, at the end of Evensong, we move to Poets' Corner with Wilde's grandson, Merlin Holland, and Queensbury's grandson, the present Marquess, and an unusually large congregation, for the dedication of a panel in the new memorial window in which all future writers' memorials will be placed, the walls and floor being full. Dame Judi Dench and Michael Denison read part of the 'handbag' scene from *The Importance*; then Sir John Gielgud, with some emotion and heard in a profound stillness, reads extracts from *De Profundis*, Oscar Wilde's letter to Lord Alfred Douglas written in Reading Gaol.

> There is only one thing for me now, absolute humility: just as there is only one thing for you, absolute humility also. You had better come down into the dust and learn it beside me.

Then Seamus Heaney gives a fine poet's address. He speaks of Wilde's 'heady paradoxes', 'his high-wire word-play' that was so effective a weapon in his hand against hypocrisy.

> The lighter his touch, the more devastating his effect. When he walked on air, he was on solid ground. That is why a window, 'that little patch of blue that prisoners call the sky', is such an appropriate memorial. A window that is the sky's threshold, not just a . . . means of illumination . . . but a poetic image as well.

I speak of one other man who deserves remembering tonight: the Reverend Stewart Headlam. It was Headlam who stood bail for Wilde, and it was Headlam who met him on his release from prison, protected him from the Press, and took Wilde to his own home, where he was able to change his clothes and drink his first cup of coffee for two years while they talked of Dante. I am glad there was at least one churchman who treated Wilde with courtesy and consideration.

My fascination with words is not some elitist hobby. Words are not the only tools we have with which to try to give some part of our experience a shape outside ourselves, the mould that our innermost thoughts must be pressed into if we are to share them. We have Gregorian chant and jazz and Beethoven's late quartets; we have the portraits of Rembrandt, Michelangelo's sculpture, Bernard Leach's pottery and the landscapes of Cézanne. Yet words are amazing, able to be shaped and fashioned to express every conceivable human emotion and circumstance, from the first bedtime story we hear at our mother's knee to *Anna Karenina* or a sonnet by Shakespeare. They are all we have if our invisible thoughts and feelings are to be incarnated, given substance, breath become speech, all we have with which to pass the time of day or make a declaration of love, or even share an insight about the Mystery. Each letter of the alphabet may have a power which is at times absurd. The minor Irish poet Alfred Noyes achieved some unwelcome notoriety when his poem 'All night he slept beneath the stars' was printed in the *Irish Times* as 'All night he slept beneath the stairs'.[4] But a single letter may also have an awesome and terrible power: in Nazi Germany 'even one letter – like the J [for Jew] on a passport – could have the power of life or death'.[5] The finest writers can take those letters and juggle them so skilfully that in speaking of the deepest things, in telling their story, they tell our story too – and this is where it is relevant to preaching – for if the experience of any one of us does not resonate within the common experience of humanity, then language fails. It becomes merely a private, ultimately self-indulgent waste of breath or print. For words are concerned to capture all that is deepest and most strange within us, and therefore least easy of expression. And sometimes it can happen, say in writing or reading a poem or a novel (or even a sermon) to find words that ring true of what we know in our heads about the way a bird flies, or a tree grows, or how a loved face looks; or what it feels like to look for the first time at your new-born child and see a living creature with ears and thumbs and fingernails, and a palm engraved with the unique lines he or she will carry to the grave; or about what it feels like to be in love or to be forgiven; or even about what it means to say that God is Christ-like.

In second-hand bookshops I tend to avoid the section marked 'second-hand theology' – for that's what too much of it is, other people's quickly obsolete, second-hand ideas about God. I make instead for the novelists, the poets and the dramatists, for the best of them are able to illuminate the story of our days with fresh perception. Eliot spoke of how all great literature is our contemporary, transcending its own time and place by the timeless quality of its language and the timeless nature of its concerns, and none speak to us more directly than certain poets and novelists – Milton and Shakespeare, Hardy and Herbert and Blake, Tolstoy and Dickens, Jane Austen and George Eliot – of what human is and could be; of pain, love and self-sacrifice, of guilt, forgiveness and transfiguration. 'The artist', writes Joseph Conrad, 'speaks to the sense of mystery surrounding our lives: to our sense of pity and beauty and pain.'[6] And in his Preface to *The Nigger of the Narcissus* he writes of the writer's and painter's art as being

a single-minded attempt to render the highest kind of justice to the visible universe . . . to find in its forms, in its colours, in its light, in the aspects of matter and in the facts of life, what of each is fundamental, what is enduring and essential – their one illuminating and convincing quality – the very truth of their existence . . . My task is, by the power of the written word, to make you hear, to make you feel – it is, before all, to make you *see*. That – and no more, and it is everything.[7]

When a writer succeeds in doing that, 'it *is* everything', and it should astonish us. And we come to understand that to ask 'What is literature, what is poetry (or art, or music)?' is another way of asking 'What is a human being?'

That is why poets and novelists are honoured in Poets' Corner and musicians across on the other side of the Abbey in Musicians' Aisle. It is because they come closer than most of us to capturing in words or sounds the mystery of a world in which matter is the bearer of spirit. In words placed on a page in a certain sequence by Hopkins or Keats, in notes and chords marked on a score in this order and not that by Bach or Haydn, we are put in touch with that which transcends the sayable in those mysteries we call poetry and music. Put in touch with that indefinable 'beyond-ness' at the heart of things. Emily Dickinson, that intensely private and passionate woman, has her own characteristically distinctive definition of poetry:

If I read a book and it makes my whole body so cold no fire can ever warm me, I know that is poetry. If I feel physically as if the top of my head were taken off, I know that is poetry. These are the only ways I know it. Is there any other way?[8]

Memorable words, yet they leave us with questions as to why there should be

this stuff called poetry and music . . . which strikes our heart at such a magic angle? And why there should be certain things in this random universe which cry out to us with their loveliness. And why it should be poetry that captures them.[9]

The only answer that begins to make sense (to fall back on a snippet of that second-hand theology I so rashly dismissed) is that ours is an incarnational world created by an incarnational God: that is to say, one whose presence is to be discerned in the stuff of the universe. That ours is a world in which not only (in R. S. Thomas' words) 'matter is the scaffolding of spirit',[10] but in which the holy is revealed in the ordinary (if anything whose component parts, the cells and nuclei and atoms, bonding together to form slugs and apricots and human flesh, may be considered 'ordinary'); and the ordinary is far more extraordinary than we think. Every serious work of art is a kind of incarnation: a visible enfleshing of an invisible thought or insight, the immeasurable translated into the measurable; or an attempt to capture in imprecise, approximate words that which in the end eludes our grasp. For words have their own little solar system of meanings, and even the simplest things can defy description. 'That crow flying across', writes Ted Hughes

how are we going to give an account of . . . [its] flight? It is not enough to say it flies purposefully, or heavily, or rowingly, or whatever. There are no words to capture the depth of *crowiness* in a crow's flight . . . The ominous thing in the flight, the barefaced, bandit thing, the tattered beggarly gipsy thing, the caressing and shaping yet slightly clumsy gesture of the down-stroke, as if the wings were both too heavy and too powerful, and the headlong sort of merriment, the macabre pantomime ghoulishness and the undertaker sleekness – you could go on for a very long time with phrases like that and still have completely missed your instant, glimpsed knowledge of the crow's wingbeat. And a bookload of such description is immediately rubbish when you see the crow flying . . . rising beyond the range of language.[11]

Yet if we are to communicate the truth to one another, or explore the mystery that lies at each of our centres, and the deeper mystery of the being of God, words are all we have. There is language and there is silence. There are words, and there is the space between them. In many ways our century, despite some incomparable writers, has seen a disintegration of language, a kind of withering of that 'internal' language – personal, human language that addresses people as people and comes from the heart – and the growth of its opposite:

69

an 'external' language so down-graded by jargon and gener-
ality, so concerned to be free of personal bias or human
considerations, that it is destructive of the common life. By
contrast, there is the powerful language of many writers this
century in the old Soviet Union and Eastern Europe. Paul
Celan was born into a Jewish family in Romania. His parents
were taken to a concentration camp and perished there. Of
the long midnight of Europe he wrote:

Only one thing remained reachable, close and secure amid all losses:
language . . . But it had to pass through its own unresponsiveness,
pass through its own fearful muting, pass through the thousand
darknesses of death-bringing speech. It went through. It gave me
no words for what was happening, but went through it. Went
through, and could resurface . . . In this language I tried, during
those years and the years after, to write poems: in order to speak,
to orient myself, to find out where I was, where I was going, to
chart my reality.[12]

Such people, often fearfully oppressed and with no certainty
that they will survive, are true to their vision of what it
means to be human and stake out for us the necessary par-
ameters of the human spirit. Like people returning from the
dead 'they have an improved perception, an unerring sense
of what really counts in being alive'.[13] As Seamus Heaney
writes: 'In one sense the efficacy of poetry is nil; no lyric has
ever stopped a tank. In another sense, it is unlimited. It is
like [Jesus] writing in the sand in the face of which accusers
and accused are left speechless and renewed.'[14]

It is another phrase of Seamus Heaney that is lodged in
my mind. Writing of his childhood and youth, he describes
the unforgettable moment when he first read the work of
another Irish poet, Patrick Kavanagh. Of how Kavanagh

took my familiar world and embodied it, enfleshed it, in new-
minted words. [Here was] the strange stillness and heat and solitude

of the sunlit fields, the inexplicable melancholy of distant work-sounds, all caught in a language that was familiar yet strangely new . . . Potato pits with rime on them, iced-over puddles being crunched, cows being milked, a child nicking the doorpost with a pen-knife . . . All at once I knew the primitive delight in finding world become word.[15]

'World become word'. Those remembered in Poets' Corner lie there because their restless, lifelong ambition was to render the visible world in words. They took our familiar world and 'embodied it, enfleshed it, in new-minted words', words which were an expression of themselves and came from the heart. Books, sermons, political speeches which do not come from the heart fall on stony ground. And if I want to persuade you that everything I've written so far are the best words I can find to convey the truth that is in me, I will say: 'I give you my word.' Give it in two senses. For I mean that I want to share with you a thought, a feeling, that resonates in my own being and that I find illuminating because it seems to me to be true; I want to take something that lies at my own centre, something that makes me *me*, and share it with you. In offering you 'my word' I offer you something of myself, but unless this is a real self-giving that costs something in time and effort, and unless you give me something costly of yourself in return – your attention – then there is no real meeting and nothing has been shared. There will just have been a small disturbance in the air, as if a flight of birds had passed overhead on their way to roost elsewhere.

The second meaning of 'I give you my word' is 'You can trust me. I give you my word, my word of honour.' Part of the disintegration of language is the loss of integrity at this deeper level, the common disease of word-breaking. For language is cheapened, and the community is weakened, unless we honour two principles: that of trust, that is to say, standing by your word; and that of truthfulness, that is to say, the use of words that say what they mean and mean what they say, words that can be stood by. And to give one's word is to speak where we stand – and afterwards we shall stand in the presence of what we have said. Nowhere is this more true than in marriage: that mutual and unconditional giving of one's word into an unknown future.

Now, if it is true that we most truly communicate with each other by revealing something of our own inner being, that is to say, by giving our word, then it must be true of the God in whose image we are made. So Genesis tells of a God who speaks out of a profound silence and says: 'Let there be light!' 'In the beginning was the Word.' In the words of the Psalmist: 'By the word of the Lord were the heavens made, by the breath of his mouth all the heavenly hosts ... For he spoke and it came to pass, he commanded and it stood fast.'[16] And as chaos gives way to order, the morning stars sing together and all the sons of God shout for joy because time has begun, a story has begun. And over aeons of time God (as it were) sings his creation into being, sings into being wild roses and snakes, mountains and rivers and the great blue whale, each creature named and assigned its place. 'I give you my Word', says God, as civilisations rise and fall, until in time there emerges a particular nation, Israel, and within that nation prophetic men who are responsive to his Word, and through his grace proclaim it.

But the words of life fall on deaf ears until, in a new and spectacular way, God says: 'I give you my Word: I give you myself.' The Word is the chosen way in which God intervenes in his creation and through which he reveals himself. And so St John, bringing to the story of the birth of Jesus the deep insight of a poet, says not 'once upon a time a baby was born' but 'the Word was made flesh and dwelt among us, full of grace and truth.' The Word: the Logos. God's action in the life of Jesus was not some divine afterthought, but his timeless purpose, the meaning of the universe embodied in a human life. This Word, says St John, tells of God just as your words tell of who you are. It has God in it just as your words have you in them, just as they contain your breath and your own unique feel. Here is all the truth about God we need to know and it is full of wonder, the secret of the universe revealed first in the cry of a new-born child, 'the Word', in Lancelot Andrewes' phrase, 'who cannot speak a word'; then in human words and actions that console, astonish and offend in equal measure; then in the bloody, pain-racked body of the man hanging on a cross and speaking words of forgiveness and desolation.

For Seamus Heaney the revelation came when in the poetry of Patrick Kavanagh he discovered 'the primitive delight of *world become word*' and his most profound childhood experiences are given a universal authenticity. For us, the moment of revelation is also the opposite. Here is nothing less than the earthing of God in his creation, not simply world become word, but the Word made flesh, or *Word become world*, the very essence of God become flesh like our flesh, speaking words and performing actions which are recognised as having a universal authenticity. Here is the Word that informs and is also dynamic, bringing men and women face to face with the living God. It enters into history. It is tender, yet charged with explosive power. From this moment everything must be redefined. Everything, starting with God. For here is God giving us the essence of himself in the only terms we can understand, a God who in Jesus is saying: 'But I am not like that: I am like this.' God revealed as Christ-like.

So God's self-portrait, God's Word, turns out to be more ordinary and more extraordinary than anyone had dreamed. As ordinary as the man working in the village carpenter's shop and stumbling on the road to Calvary, or sharing that human desolation when God seems to have deserted us; as extraordinary as every human being made in the divine image is shown by this man to be, if and when we turn and open ourselves to the life-changing, transfiguring power of the Father's love.

Words matter. Words can heal and they can destroy. They can change lives. They can reveal something more of the mystery we are. When I give you my considered word I give you a truth that lies deep at my centre and which I want to share with you. So does God in his Word made flesh. But I also give you my word of honour: I say that you can believe me. Which is, of course, God's meaning too. For in Jesus Christ, who knew what it was to live, to suffer and to die, he is saying: 'Trust me. I give you my word that you are loved. Even when that seems unlikely or even impossible; even when life is at its darkest and most perverse. I am the God who is beside you and whose life is within you: beside you whether you believe or whether you doubt, when you are content and when you are depressed, when you grieve and when you rejoice, at all times and in all places; and beside you eventually in your dying and through and beyond your death. Trust me. I give you my Word.'

In the beginning was the Word, and it is the Word that gives life. But in the end there is silence. The silence when all our halting, approximate words, even the finest and most memorable of them, come to an end. The books are shut. Poets' Corner closes for the night. And in the ensuing silence two things remain. Gratitude; and wonder.

God our Father,
you sent your son, Jesus, the Word made flesh,
to live among us and to proclaim your love and forgiveness
        for all;
give us grace to listen to his voice,
that it may give meaning to our lives
and that we may continue to bear witness to the Word
                in all we say and all we are;
and this we ask through the same Jesus Christ our Lord.

6

LENT IV

The West Front

On self-giving love; and on our proper end

Almighty Father,
whose Son was revealed in majesty
   before he suffered death upon the cross:
give us faith to perceive his glory,
that we may be strengthened to suffer with him
and be changed into his likeness, from glory to glory;
who is alive and reigns with you and the Holy Spirit,
one God, now and for ever.

Suffering was no stranger to John Clare or Oscar Wilde. Clare described himself as 'a lost man'. When he escapes in 1841 from Matthew Allen's aylum he writes to his first and life-long love, the already dead Mary Jones, that he feels 'homeless at home'. A schizophrenic incarcerated in institutions for the second half of his life, Clare in his last years writes the moving sonnet 'I am – yet what I am, none cares or knows'.[1] Oscar Wilde, being transferred from Pentonville to Reading Gaol on a rainy November afternoon in 1895, stands handcuffed and in prison clothing for half an hour on the platform at Clapham Junction where a crowd begins to form, first laughing and then jeering at him. It must have seemed an eternity. One man recognises him and spits in his face. 'For a year after that was done to me', wrote Wilde, 'I wept every day at the same hour and for the same space of time.'[2]

For Jesus the suffering is both different and the same.

75

Different in that he suffered and died in order to maintain the integrity of his cause, to keep faith with the Father, to be the love of God to the bitter end. Yet also the same, for he too knew, in Gethsemane and on Golgotha, human anguish and fear and the pain of betrayal and of nails tearing his flesh. Life has never been fair. It is always unpredictable and sometimes dangerous. To be human means to be vulnerable and Jesus was no exception. His world was equally full of spiritually blind and worldly people. He too was unsure about what each new day might bring. For him, it brought a cross. He knew what most of us can only faintly imagine: what it is like to face arrest, to be condemned at a fixed trial, to be tortured, spat upon and jeered at as you hang dying. Yet if what we see at Calvary is the human face of God, the manner in which what we call the Passion reveals God's heart of compassion, then it reveals that our human suffering need not be a nonsense and a waste. For this is the point at which the divine story and the human story are most powerfully linked. In the words of Timothy Rees' fine hymn:

> Wherever love is outraged,
>   wherever hope is killed,
> where man still wrongs his brother man,
>   thy Passion is fulfilled.

The Church's chief task is to be the living reminder in every age of the divine story, a reminder in its annual recounting of the stories of Christmas, Holy Week, Easter and Pentecost, names which describe how the Christ-like God has acted within the confines of history. Actions which are definitive for all future time, but which are spelled out in the homely language of one man's life and teaching and healing, and loving and forgiving, and suffering and dying. Our task is to make connections between his story and ours, between our little lives and the great life of God within us, but also (for example, and more remarkably) between our sufferings and God's suffering in Jesus Christ. For not only is that connection one of the central truths on which Christian belief rests, it is also the most comforting and affirming reality, and the starting-point in finding a way to turn whatever suffering we may have to face to creative ends.

Yet there is a more subtle form of suffering implicit in that 'suffering with' Christ the collect would have us ask for, and in what Jesus meant when he invited his followers to 'take up your cross and follow me'. A form of suffering that is not caused by illness or accident or anything imposed upon us from outside, but which is *self-chosen*. What we call Christ's Passion was anything but passive. He embraced it, in the sense that there was no other way in which he could witness to the truth that was in him, and ever since there have been men and women who have stood for the truth (as they have perceived it) against the lie even to the point of torture and death. In the nave of the Abbey there still stands the Tudor pulpit from which Archbishop Thomas Cranmer preached at the funeral of his godson, the young King Edward VI, in the presence of the Catholic Queen Mary. In that instantly changed climate, he must have felt more than a shuddering premonition of his own approaching passion and death at the stake.

Four centuries later another archbishop, Janani Luwum of Uganda, courageously opposed the evil actions of Idi Amin and was quickly found murdered. A third archbishop, Oscar Romero of El Salvador, wrote and preached against a heartless regime and took the side of the poor and the oppressed. He was not prepared to be muzzled by the government, and he predicted the likelihood of his own sudden death; within a few days he was shot at the altar while celebrating Mass in his cathedral. As I write, another bishop has been murdered: Juan Gerardi Conedera of Guatemala. Part of his diocese became the scene of the most tragic and blood-stained period of modern Guatemalan history. Thousands of impoverished Mayan Indians were terrorised, and socially committed Christians, many of them priests, were marked as subversives and killed. In 1980 Bishop Gerardi took the unprecedented step of closing down his diocese and going into exile. Eventually he returned and set up a project, The Recovery of Historical Memory, an attempt to record the atrocities that the country had endured. Just after Easter this year its findings were published. Two days later Juan Gerardi was bludgeoned to death. In the words of his obituarist: 'He was left faceless, like tens of thousands of victims of the war'.[3] In July 1998 statues to Luwum and Romero, together with eight other twentieth-century martyrs, were placed in the empty niches on the west front of the Abbey.

A handful of Christians become martyrs because they place obedience to God's authority above the authority of a dictatorship or an inhumane regime; many men and women of all faiths and none are Christ-like in their refusal to compromise their integrity even when the alternative is imprisonment without trial, house arrest or a bullet in the back of the head. For the past decade there has stood at the entrance to the nave of the Abbey a lighted candle, one with barbed wire twisting round it to signify those who are imprisoned for conscience' sake. Each week a new name, supplied by Amnesty International, is placed beside the candle, recording the details of this man or that woman languishing in some fetid prison in one of the nations where human rights are violated, perhaps one of those where torture is still common, and he or she is prayed for daily at one of the eucharists.

For most of us, however, the way will be much less dramatic: as humdrum, yet as costly, as small acts of love and forgiveness. For example:

Good Friday 1988

Three wooden crosses have been made in Londonderry, site of Bloody Sunday. Two have gone to Belfast and Dublin to be the centre of acts of prayer for healing and forgiveness; one has come to London. Today at 5 p.m., after the singing of the Passion and the Three Hour meditation on the words from the Cross, five hundred people join a silent procession of witness and penitence from Westminster (Roman Catholic) Cathedral to the Abbey, one man carrying the cross. We clear the nave of all chairs and all crowd in, filling the space and standing shoulder to shoulder. There are three Bible readings by those of different traditions, and then a short, simple confession of past wrongs and present division by an Irish Roman Catholic, an Irish Protestant and an Englishman, each in their own words. We sing a Taizé chant, and then join in an unaccompanied singing of 'When I survey the wondrous Cross'. We then exchange the Peace, and afterwards there is a spontaneous burst of applause. Afterwards I take a few people to see the stone that lies beside the white marble tomb erected by James I for Queen Elizabeth. In the vault beneath there is just room for her coffin which lies on top of that of her half-sister Queen Mary. On the tomb the Latin inscription reads: 'Partners both in throne and grave, here rest we two sisters, Elizabeth and Mary, in the hope of one resurrection'; and beside it a floor-stone unveiled in 1977 commemorates those who, divided at the Reformation, 'laid down their lives for Christ and conscience' sake'.

St Patrick's Day 1993

The community of Corrymeela, at Ballycastle on the Antrim coast, has for 30 years been witnessing to reconciliation, providing a sanctuary for those damaged by the unhealed wound that is Northern Ireland and a meeting place for all sides in this fractured society. Tonight members of the community and their friends come for an ecumenical service of thanksgiving and prayer in the quire. They set up a rough wooden cross before the high altar, and the moving climax is a simple dance illustrating the pain of divided people brought together at the foot of the reconciling cross. We hear of other ecumenical communities whose silent, costly work never hits the headlines but will have contributed enormously to any final establishment of peace, like the one set up 25 years ago near the Shankill Road in Belfast, two of whose members – one Catholic, one Protestant – have together visited the homes of the bereaved following a sectarian murder and attended the funeral of the victims.

In this week's collect we ask for **'faith to perceive his glory, that we may be strengthened to suffer with him and be changed into his likeness, from glory to glory'.** The Psalmist speaks of God's house as being the place 'where thy glory dwells',[4] and our minds vaguely conjure up a sense of the numinous, an awesome space; yet when John wants just one word to describe the lasting impact the life and death of Jesus had made on those closest to him, that's the unexpected word he seizes on: 'we saw his glory'. If you had asked, 'Where chiefly did you see his glory?' I guess John might have replied that they saw it chiefly when he was hanging on the cross and when, a few hours earlier, he had knelt at the supper table to wash their feet. And not just the glory of Jesus but the glory of God. For cross and foot-washing are the ultimate demonstration of that suffering, self-giving love which they now see to lie at God's heart. At first this seems a topsy-turvy, Humpty-Dumpty kind of definition of 'glory',[5] until you get the point, until you fathom the values of the Kingdom, where the first are last and the last first, where the just law of 'an eye for an eye' is countermanded by the compassionate gospel of forgiveness, and where greatness lies in the often menial and costly service of others. This is why Paul can speak of seeing 'the glory of God in the face of Jesus Christ'.[6] The writers of Genesis tell us that we are created in God's image, but looking at the world around us (or even at the world within) it is often hard to believe it. We need, as it were, a new template. In Jesus we have it. Here is the true and undistorted image of God in man: here is the glory of what all human beings are created to be. And if we are prepared to be open to his Spirit (that Holy Spirit who is so often referred to by Paul as the Spirit of Christ), we ourselves may begin to be changed – painfully slowly, and over a lifetime – into our true likeness. 'All of us . . . seeing the glory of the Lord . . . are being transformed into his likeness with ever-increasing glory, through the power of the Lord who is the Spirit.'[7]

'What do I really want?' That's the abiding question, spoken or unspoken, that dogs us down the years. For each of us an answer of sorts manifests itself in the job I've chosen, the role I play, the possessions with which I surround myself, the value I put on people and things. It is fed in as the grain of ambition and desire; it emerges as the wheat of achievements (or the weeds of frustration). But ask that question in another context, see it not just against the background of my own self-centred desires and longings but in the wider sweep of that giving attention to God (which we call prayer) and that giving attention to others (which we call love), and it becomes a question about the whole purpose of my life. Does it have an end, a design, an objective? Can it be true that the whole motive of my life, its ultimate purpose, is to grow in the likeness of Jesus, living out his attitudes and desiring his objectives: that is to say, growing in the power to love?

My fault throughout my ministry – if it is a fault – has been to focus too much on speaking, preaching, counselling, on the loving-kindness of God, his compassion and mercy, at the expense of his majesty and judgement; on the loving, affirming words of Jesus at the cost of his severe and solemn ones. At an unconscious level that probably has much to do with my own story, my own search for a father's love, my own need for affirmation; yet I have done so consciously and deliberately because many people's apprehension of the Christian faith is often minimal, at best hazily remembered from childhood, at worst bizarrely distorted by an extreme fundamentalism. Thomas Merton warns of those who would use fear to convert people and make the Gospel the exclusive preserve of the chosen few:

The magicians keep turning the Cross to their own purposes . . . saying that Christ has locked all the doors, has given one answer, settled everything and departed, leaving all life enclosed in the frightful consistency of a system outside of which there is [only] . . . damnation, [and] inside of which there is the intolerable flippancy of the saved – while nowhere is there any place left for the mystery of the freedom of the divine mercy.[8]

There is a severity about many of Jesus' words, but the fiercest are addressed to those religious leaders who draw strict boundaries between 'us' and 'them', whose obsession with the letter of the Law is stifling the spirit; and the whole impetus of his words and actions is the tenacious love God has for his world and every person in it, not least the socially unacceptable and the outcast. The persistent love we see enfleshed in Jesus at once corrects and completes whatever else may be said of God and his relationship with his world.

I have touched in an earlier chapter on the other reason why my scales have been so weighted on one side: a growing recognition of the loneliness that so many people feel, the vulnerability that always underlies even the most phlegmatic British exterior, and the hunger of the human spirit for some meaning and some kind of vision. Westminster Abbey may seem a daunting building, yet a good number of unhappy or disturbed individuals are drawn to it – as they are to every large church or cathedral which promises that kind of unthreatening anonymity which parish churches cannot so easily provide. And what they most want is someone to reassure them that they have an absolute value in God's sight. (Which is why there is never any moment of the day when a priest is not present in the Abbey, ready to listen, advise or absolve.) I think of just one of them. John was an accountant, but increasingly he succumbed to long bouts of illness. He knew times of confusion and pain; sometimes (like so many) he despaired. It was a real sharing of the cross. At other times he had a single-minded, child-like perception which could be startling. He wrote poetry and loved music, and was by nature kind and gentle. And he loved the Abbey passionately. For the last years of his life he spent an increasing amount of time sitting in the nave or the cloisters or St Faith's Chapel, soaking up the atmosphere of the ever-changing building.

John developed cancer and for several months was cared for in a London hospice. Three weeks before he died he wrote me a letter which simply said: 'A good man crucified is a cruelty exposed. A cruelty forgiven is divine. John.' A week later, when I visited him, he handed me this:

Death is becoming a little noisy, a little too obvious . . . What should I say? How am I to face this knocking? I realise I must go to the door and look this person in the eye . . . With good luck the stranger will not cause me pain. But when does the moment come? As I turn the key or beyond on the threshold? We believe it is God who knocks and I trust this is so. Anyway, I shall go to the door quite soon and I must not keep him waiting. John.[9]

He died in early January. We gave him a funeral service in the Lady Chapel, where throughout the previous night his coffin had been covered by the embroidered pall used both for monarchs and members of the Abbey family, united by 'Pale Death [who] kicks his way equally into the cottages of the poor and the castles of kings'.[10]

When death comes
like the hungry bear in autumn;
when death comes and takes all the bright
    coins from his purse . . .

83

I want to step through the door full of curiosity, wondering:
what is it going to be like, that cottage of darkness?

And therefore I look upon everything
as a brotherhood and a sisterhood . . .

and I think of each life as a flower, as common
as a field daisy, and as singular,

and each name a comfortable music in the mouth,
tending, as all music does, toward silence . . .

When it's over, I want to say: all my life
I was a bride married to amazement.
I was the bridegroom, taking the world into my arms.

When it's over, I don't want to wonder
if I made of my life something particular, and real.
I don't want to find myself sighing and frightened,
or full of argument.

I don't want to end up simply having visited this world.[11]

Lines from a poem by the American poet Mary Oliver bring
me back to the question of the purpose of our lives. Most of
our lives are about doing: they should also be about being
and becoming. For we have this extraordinary capacity, the
capacity to love, to give ourselves in love and to delight in
receiving it; and our destiny as lovers-in-the-making is to
share (if we desire it) in 'the Love which moves the sun and
the other stars',[12] which is none other than God himself. We
are programmed for nothing less. This is why we are restless,
homesick, aware of a sense of incompleteness and dissatis-
faction, and – strangest of all – aware too of an altruistic
desire to reach out to others, to go beyond the narrow world
of our own self-concern. In Thomas Traherne's *Centuries*, he

writes of how each of us 'is as prone to love as the sun is to shine', and adds: 'Never was anything in this world loved too much, but many things have been loved in a false way: and all in too short a measure.'[13]

During the past two evenings I have by chance watched films that each witness to the power of a persisting human love that is beyond all reason. The first was *Dead Man Walking*, which tells the true story of Sister Helen Préjean who first corresponded with, and then visited, a death-cell inmate in one of the American states where the law for murder is still based on the ancient Holiness Code, the *lex talionis*, the law of retaliation ('an eye for an eye'), rather than the Gospel realities of repentance, forgiveness and atonement. The murder could not have been more vicious, nor the murderer less appealing; yet Sister Helen (in the face of much angry opposition and at great personal cost) stays with him for his final weeks and accompanies him until in the death cell the injected poison does its work. The second film, in total contrast, was Richard Eyre's television production of *King Lear*. Lear longs not simply to be loved but to be given proof of it, yet is unprepared to let others see his vulnerability as well as his strength. As has been pointed out, the Fool provokes Lear and Edgar provokes both Lear and his own father, Gloucester, in an attempt to nurse the two tormented old men back to sanity and this is an act of love, 'while Goneril and Regan speak to Lear in tones of the coldest rationality, trying to check his anguished demands [not with love but] with reason'.[14]

So often, in counselling individuals, I have felt great empathy with those who face that common human problem of seemingly unreasonable elderly parents. I have come to understand – a bit late in the day – how wasted my own attempts to reason with my own remarkable but emotionally demanding mother have been. I have reasoned with her seeming unreasonableness and felt angry at it. I should have realised that, having been widowed three times and with a great need for love, she did not want reason but reassurance. Now, in her confused old age, I feel a new compassion.[15]

Aristotle believed that the most fundamental cause of anything is its end, its destiny, and that the end is there in the beginning, implicit in its very nature. The end for children is adult life; the end for adults is the maturity (and hopefully wisdom) won from a lifetime's experience – and, perhaps, a growing curiosity about their ultimate destiny; the end for this chapter, implicit from the beginning, is to define what that destiny might be. For whereas reason tells me to 'remember you are dust, and to dust you shall return', other clues point me to a different answer. They point to home. In a book called *The Longing for Home* the American writer Frederick Buechner tells of his search for 'the home I long for every day of my life', and

I believe that in my heart I have found, and have maybe always known, the way that leads to it. I believe that the home we long for and belong to is finally where Christ is. I believe that home is Christ's kingdom, which exists both within us and among us as we wend our prodigal ways through the world in search of it.[16]

If, as Paul claims, our true homeland is in heaven, how are we to speak of that which is literally unimaginable other than in some such quickly tedious practice as that of 'casting down our golden crowns about the glassy sea'? My mind tells me that I can't do so; my heart tells me something different. That somehow the meaning of heaven is linked to the two most important lessons we have to learn on earth: how to trust and how to love. Learning to trust that the hunger I sometimes feel is not for anything money can buy, but for the bringing to fruition of that potential for love, those stirrings of compassion, that longing for justice, that response to beauty, those intimations of joy, that have prompted me all my life in my search for God, and drawn me inevitably, as iron filings are drawn to magnetic north, in the direction of home. And that one day that hunger will be satisfied. In her remarkable novel about the Holocaust, *Fugitive Pieces*, Anne Michaels writes:

In experiments to determine the mechanisms of migration, scientists locked warblers in cages and kept them in darkened rooms where they couldn't see the sky. The birds lived in bewildered twilight. Yet each October, they huddled, agitated, turned inside out with yearning. The magnetic pole pulled their blood, the thumbprint of night sky on their inner eye.[17]

To hope for heaven (or the Kingdom or the City of God, call it what we will) is simply to set our hunger in the context of eternity.

Our end is to find rest at last from our fussy self-centredness, anxiety and self-concern; to see truths about our own value and each other's value in God's sight which will set us free to love. I cannot believe we shall lose our separate identities, merged like drops of water in some amorphous sea. Rather, we shall still be our unique, irreplaceable selves; and those words of the lover to the beloved, 'I love you because you are you', a truth implied in every encounter of Jesus with an individual in need, will describe God's relationship with each one of us for ever. That for me is what alone rings true as I reflect on the meaning and mystery of my life and death; rings true to the promises of Jesus; rings true to everything I have learned about the nature of love; rings true to my own experience of loving and being loved; and rings true to my own deepest instincts that the essence of love is to affirm the right of the beloved to exist. In Jesus God does just that. He affirms each one of us in all the mystery of our being. And what God affirms nothing can contradict or deny. That is the hope that gives meaning to a world which on bad days we may feel to be hopeless; the hope with which Christians faced the last millennium and with which we face the new one.

It would astonish me to be told that many of the things that touch me most deeply reflect only my own mind and heart. For what makes biographies so satisfying is the discovery of the general in the particular. We share a story which is both unique and the same. What Christians claim is that there is a greater story which resonates in all our spoken and unspoken stories and pulls them together and makes sense of them. A story that hangs upon the two poles of creation and redemption, that tells of suffering and glory. And I believed that the Abbey's task (and the task of every other Church on earth) was to enable people to see the connection between the two. So here is a small parable.

Now that I am retired I go early almost every morning to a holy space at the far end of Salisbury Cathedral called the Trinity Chapel. The east window, made in Chartres by Gabriel Loire, is dedicated to prisoners of conscience. Its three central lancets present Jesus as a prisoner of conscience whose stand for truth to the point of crucifixion has inspired and strengthened those men and women all over the world who challenge the lie in whatever form and face torture and death in their own stand for truth and justice. At first, in the bleak winter months, no light penetrates the window and it appears as a darkly monochrome jigsaw of indecipherable glass. But gradually, as morning prayer begins, the dawn light seeps through the glass and the first colour to appear is glass of the palest blue: glass in the shape of a long widening triangle stemming from the head of the cross on which the body of Jesus hangs, and this extended blue triangle lights up the faces of the prisoners, some holding crosses, some held in symbolic chains, in the lower part of the window. The next colour to appear is a blood-red crimson. It surrounds the hanging body of Jesus. It finds echoes in some of the prisoners' clothing. Finally, as the Eucharist gets under way, a shower of gold appears at the very apex of the window above the crucified, gold suggesting the glory of the self-giving love of God as that is seen in the suffering and death of Jesus; gold that also speaks of resurrection.

Blue and crimson and gold. I do not know of any modern work of art which more successfully connects our human story, the story (at its most testing) of those men and women who even now endure what Dietrich Bonhoeffer called 'the suffering of God in the life of the world', to that most powerful story of all, the story that can both strengthen and change us as the pattern of our own journey continues to unfold.

Almighty Father,
whose Son was revealed in majesty
  before he suffered death upon the cross:
give us faith to perceive his glory,
that glory revealed in a life of self-giving,
that we may be strengthened to suffer with him
in costly acts of generous love,
and be changed into his likeness, from glory to glory;
who is alive and reigns with you and the Holy Spirit,
one God, now and for ever.

7

LENT V

The Innocent Victims' Memorial

On remembering the innocent

Most merciful God,
who by the death and resurrection of your Son Jesus Christ
delivered and saved mankind:
grant that by faith in him who suffered on the cross, we
**   may triumph**
in the power of his victory;
through Jesus Christ our Lord

I am writing this book during Lent 1998, tackling a chapter
a week, keeping pace with the season as it evolves. Yesterday
we entered the two weeks of Passiontide. The Passion was
the crown and goal of Jesus' life, the Passion story the oldest
part of the Gospel tradition to receive a definite shape.
Although the English words 'passion' and 'patience' are
derived from the Greek word meaning 'to suffer', in Greek
the word also has the sense of being subject to wounds and
pressures from without; it could not have been applied to a
divine being who, in Greek thought, was remote and self-
sufficient. That is not the Christian concept of God, and in
old French and early Middle English the word 'passion' is
always used of (indeed, restricted to) Christ's suffering on
the cross, as it is in the Wycliffe and other early English
versions of the Bible. The King James version of 1611,
however, only retains the word once: in the opening verses
of Acts which speak of Christ showing himself alive 'after
his passion'. For us the word more commonly has the

meaning of a strongly felt emotion, sometimes anger, often love. Which is fitting, for nowhere is Jesus more powerful than in his passive suffering on the cross. Nowhere is the passionate love of God more strikingly revealed. And today nowhere is Christ's passion more visible than in the innocent victims of our world. 'Innocent' in the sense that they are culpable of no offence, yet wounded, betrayed, tortured, raped, made homeless or ruthlessly killed.

We cannot begin to imagine the scale of that suffering. Our minds seize up at the thought of millions of war victims and refugees; or tens of thousands of prisoners of conscience. But (unless our God-given, Godlike compassion has died in us) we cannot but respond to the dead look in the eyes of a child in a Romanian orphanage; to the thought of a youth in a rat-infested cell in some dictatorship, facing torture and crying in the night for his mother; to the photograph of Hocine, the distraught mother of eight slaughtered children in an Algerian village. We feel defeated by the enormity of the world's pain. Yet we can do something. 'He who would do good to another', wrote William Blake, 'must do it in Minute Particulars',[1] and we are forced to be rightly selective in our giving and caring and praying: loyal, and persistently loyal, to our chosen charity or charities. But we can do something else. We can remember. Not just the Unknown Warrior, but the Unknown Sufferer. And I want to write about just one day in the Abbey's life: 10 October 1996.

One day, four years earlier, we were on holiday in northern Italy, in a village high in the Dolomites which is as close as you can get to heaven. It was a morning in June, and the woods in which we walked were dappled with sunlight and full of violet snowbells and blue gentians, the meadows rich with pasque flowers. A few days earlier the headlines had been full of a massacre in which children and old people had been mutilated and killed, an event destined to be forgotten all too soon. Suddenly I knew that there had to be an Abbey memorial for those I could only think of as the innocent victims. It would not compete with the Grave of the Unknown Warrior, or question the sacrifice made by service men and women in defence of freedom: it would complement it.

My colleagues on Chapter responded warmly to the idea, and we quickly found a fine Irish sculptor, Ken Thompson from County Cork. Nothing ever goes entirely smoothly. There were months of discussion, planning applications, frustration and encouragement. But finally all were agreed that a handsome circular stone in green Cumberland slate, surrounded by a square of York stone paving, should be placed in the forecourt outside the main west doors of the Abbey, a short distance from the Unknown Warrior, but in the most public place. The lettering was to read: *Remember all innocent victims of oppression, violence and war*, with round the edge those words from the Book of Lamentation – words later applied to the crucified Jesus – *'Is it nothing to you all you who pass by?'* Dominating the stone, larger than all the rest, would be the one word *'Remember'*.

The Queen agreed to unveil the stone. We were keen that there should be in the congregation representatives of the many charitable bodies concerned with humanitarian aid and victim support, both national and international, together with asylum-seekers and former refugees who have found sanctuary in Britain. But we also wanted a score of those who had personal experience of the worst excesses of our century to accompany the Queen when she left the nave to unveil the memorial, and Baroness Lynda Chalker, at that time the Minister for Overseas Development, was invaluable in providing names.

Illustration of the Innocent Victims' Memorial by its sculptor, Kenneth Thompson.

10 October 1996

A golden autumn day. The nave is full, all the chairs turned to face the west doors. Just before noon the Queen and Prince Philip arrive. Their seats are in the front row, beside the Unknown Warrior's Grave and opposite those who will accompany them outside. After a welcome we sing Dietrich Bonhoeffer's hymn 'People draw near to God in their distress', with its potent last verse:

> And God draws near to people in distress.
> Feeding their souls and bodies with his bread;
> Christian or not, for both he's hanging dead,
> Forgiving, from the cross, their wickedness.

There follows a recollection of innocent sufferers, using words from Lamentations and Genesis (the murder of Abel by Cain), interspersed with the choir singing parts of Psalm 10: 'Why standest thou so far off, O Lord: and hidest thy face in the needful time of trouble?' My address seeks to link their passion with Christ's. The choir then sings Pablo Casals' setting of 'Is it nothing to you?' (*O vos omnes*): then we keep silence. There follows the reading of the words of the angel at the tomb of Jesus:

> 'Remember how he told you . . . that the Son of man must be
> delivered into the hands of sinful men, and be crucified,
> and on the third day rise.' And they remembered his words.

Then, during the choir's plainchant singing of further verses from Psalm 10, we process to the stone.

In front of the Queen walk in pairs 21 men and women. Celestin Rusengatabaro, who survived the genocide in Rwanda and lost 23 of his close relatives, represents the victims of Africa. He walks with Eldin Isovic, aged fourteen, who lost his sight and both hands during the Bosnian conflict and represents the victims of Europe. Daw Nita May, a widow who with her husband, a Member of Parliament, spent many years in prison in Burma for expressing their democratic views, represents the victims of Asia and walks with Leila Mantoura, a Christian from Jerusalem representing the Palestinian refugees. Two women from Northern Ireland walk together and embody the Roman Catholic and Protestant victims there: Maura Kiely, whose son was shot as he left Mass, and who belongs to the Cross Group (the members of which visit the bereaved in both communities), representing the Roman Catholic victims; and Joan Wilson, widow of Senator Gordon Wilson, whose daughter Marie was killed in the Enniskillen Remembrancetide bombing, walks on behalf of the Protestant victims.

They are followed by the poet Irina Ratushinskaya, who was imprisoned for four years in a Siberian labour camp, and who represents the victims of the Stalinist and post-Stalinist purges, who walks with the 89-year-old Yervant Shekerdemian, who is here on behalf of the victims of the Armenian Massacre in 1915, which he experienced as a boy, the last of the massacres by the Turks which were responsible for the death of a million-and-a-half Armenians. Then comes Fiona Eadington, teacher for 25 years at Dunblane Primary School, witnessing to all the children who are victims of violence. Anita Walfisch, inmate of both Belsen and Auschwitz, survived because as a young violinist she was chosen to play Schubert and Brahms in a quartet to the camp commandants when the business of the day was over. She represents all victims of the Holocaust, and she walks beside Edith Yengwa, a South African embodying the victims of apartheid. Behind them come Joanne Woodward, widow of a soldier killed while serving with the United Nations Protection Force in the former Yugoslavia whilst on peacekeeping duties, and Anna Schrader, Director of the Consortium for Street Children, representing all homeless and vulnerable children who live on the streets.

For now we have moved from the victims to the protectors, the carers and healers. The remarkable Helen Bamber, who sought asylum in Britain from Nazi Germany and, aged eighteen, was one of the first people to enter the liberated Belsen, now directs the Medical Foundation for the Care of Victims of Torture and is here on behalf of all torture victims among refugees and asylum seekers. David Bull, Director of Amnesty International, walks with her. Then come Philippe Lavanchy, the United Kingdom Representative of the UN High Commissioner for Refugees; Paul Ignatieff, Director of the European Regional Office of UNICEF, one of whose chief present concerns is children in danger from landmines. The Vice President of the International Federation of Red Cross and Red Crescent, Sylvia Limerick, walks with Pierre Keller of the Red Cross International Committee; and last of all comes the Chairman of its Council, Elspeth Thomas, with Martin Griffiths, Director of the UN Department of Humanitarian Affairs in Geneva.

It seems to me, as these 21 people stand around the stone in a wide horseshoe, that if each could have related his or her story they would have illuminated both the extremes of bestiality and cruelty, and the heights of greatness in the face of adversity, of which the human spirit is capable; a living reminder that there is nothing a person will not do *to* another, nothing that a person will not do *for* another. (Perhaps if at the millennium we were to choose one person to embody the spirit of the twentieth century it should be either a prisoner of conscience or a refugee.) The Queen unveils the stone and I dedicate it; then the Queen and the Duke lay a large white wreath: roses, freesia, chrysanthemums and snowberries, with sprigs of rosemary for remembrance. Unaccompanied, the choristers sing Robert Herrick's 'Litany to the Holy Spirit':

> In the hour of my distress
> when temptations me oppress,
> and when I my sins confess,
> Sweet Spirit, comfort me.

We return to the nave, and there follows a commitment to God's justice in which we pledge ourselves to working anew for the

creation of a just, humane and tolerant world-order in which all may live with dignity . . . striving to resist that use of power that is idolatrous, that form of prejudice that devalues others, the betrayal of the innocent, and the wilful or thoughtless creation of poverty and hunger.

We end the service (largely drafted by Colin Semper, who has an eye for such things) with prayers, a reading from Romans 8, and Timothy Rees' hymn 'God is Love':

> God is Love: and he enfoldeth
> all the world in one embrace;
> with unfailing grasp he holdeth
> every child of every race.
> And when human hearts are breaking
> under sorrow's iron rod,
> then they find that self-same aching
> deep within the heart of God.

That night, as it began to grow dark, I visited the stone again. On it lay the large white wreath. Beside this there were 17 single yellow roses, each bearing the name of one of the 16 children and their teacher, innocent victims in every sense, slaughtered on that March morning six months earlier in Dunblane.

Sermons do not travel well. They are spoken in a particular context to a particular congregation, and the freshest of words too quickly become stale. But to complete the story of what was for me a climactic and important day, and because it underlines a major theme of this book, here is what I said.

In the end words fail us. Language stumbles and falls silent in face of the horror and the pity. Nor can the imagination conceive the scale of the killing, the maiming, the torture and the rape, the slaughter of children and the acts of genocide. We can only picture and feel compassion for this unknown man, that woman, this child, and echo Wilfred Owen's poignant question of a young man killed in battle: 'Was it for this the clay grew tall?'[2]

A few of you here have known such horror at first hand, the few representing the many, and we are silenced by your presence. And yet, as that great crusader for justice Edmund Burke said of the French Revolution: 'Events have happened of which it is difficult to speak and impossible to be silent.'

Here before us is the most touching grave in the Abbey: that of the Unknown Warrior. How eloquently it speaks of the costliness of war. The stone to be unveiled by the Queen today is no less eloquent, though it has a different focus. Not for one instant does it diminish the force of this grave. It seeks rather to broaden our understanding of what has been done, and is being done daily in this bloodiest of centuries, to those who are our brothers and our sisters and whose blood, like that of Abel, 'cries to us from the ground'. This new stone speaks for those – so many of them women and children – who have been in the way: in the way of invading armies, pawns in a thousand messy wars. It speaks for those condemned for their beliefs, their culture or the colour of their skin; and indeed for every innocent victim of violence, each one the child of God and of untold value in his sight, and in the sight of those who love them.

The linking refrain in this short but significant service is a Jewish psalm. For the Psalms are the passionate songs and prayers that a people at the raw edge of their lives address to a God who often appears to be deaf to their pleas. And it is a psalm that Jesus of Nazareth, the one truly innocent victim, calls out of the depths of his desolation as he hangs naked on the cross: 'My God, my God, why hast thou forsaken me?' It is that apparent forsakenness of our century's many victims to which this stone draws attention and says by its very anonymity: 'I was, I am, your brother, your sister. Let me not be forsaken or forgotten. Remember me.'

But 'remember me' in what context? This new memorial, deliberately placed not within but outside the sheltering walls of the Abbey for all the world to see, is yet within the protective railings of a Christian church. And if there is any consolation in the Christian faith, any truth to place beside the reality of evil and human wickedness, it is precisely at that unlikely point where the one who hangs on the cross echoes the Psalmist's cry of desolation; but then, as he enters deep into the final darkness of death, speaks a word of trust: 'Lord, into your hands I commend my spirit.'

We have no easy answers to offer the victims of the Holocaust or the minefields of Cambodia, of Srebenica or Rwanda or Dunblane. To do that would be an inexcusable cheapening of their suffering. Suffering which seems to be the price of our human freedom. But the Christian claim is that at the heart of the mystery is the God who once in Christ became one with us in all the vulnerability of human life, and knows to the full its pain, its costliness and its desolation. As Dietrich Bonhoeffer, the German pastor executed by the Nazis, wrote from his prison cell: 'Only a suffering God can help.' If God is revealed in Christ, then that cry of desolation from the cross is the ultimate mystery of the God who so identifies himself with his creation that in Christ he too knows what it is to suffer and to die. God at one with all who for whatever reason feel engulfed by the powers of darkness.

'I am your brother, your sister. Let me not stand forsaken and forgotten. Remember me.' And that cry then takes the form of a question, a question which should quicken our compassion, the question that encircles and completes our stone, 'Is it nothing to you, all you who pass by?'

Most merciful God,
who by the death and resurrection of your Son Jesus Christ
delivered and saved mankind:
grant that by faith in him who suffered on the cross,
we may grow in compassion for those who this day
    suffer violence and oppression,

and that, together with them,
we may triumph in the power of his victory;
through Jesus Christ our Lord.

PALM SUNDAY

The Abbot's Pew

On our public and private selves;
on human rights and on dying well

Almighty and everlasting God,
who in your tender love towards mankind
　sent your Son our Saviour Jesus Christ
to take upon him our flesh
and to suffer death upon the cross:
grant that we may follow the example
　of his patience and humility,
and also be made partakers of his resurrection;
through Jesus Christ our Lord.

I have focused on most of the Abbey's familiar public spaces: nave and quire and sanctuary, Poets' Corner, St Faith's Chapel and the Shrine of St Edward, even the forecourt with its newest memorial. But there are two spaces that the public rarely see: remarkable spaces with, as it were, one foot in the Abbey and one in the house that was my home, combining public role and private person.

The more unexpected is called the Abbot's Pew. It is an integral part of the Deanery, a small wooden gallery built in Abbot Islip's time in the early sixteenth century. I would ease open a heavy door just outside my second-floor study and find myself in a room looking down unobserved on the nave thirty feet below: a unique viewpoint from which through the centuries deans must have kept an eye on things. The walls and ceiling are painted white, with the fourth side open, like a box in a theatre. Against the east wall stands a handsome oak and cherry-wood altar designed and given by Lord Linley after his wedding in St Margaret's. From the ceiling hangs an incense thurible presented by the Orthodox Ecumenical Patriarch; beneath it a Moroccan carpet presented by a visiting dignitary, covered with Islamic symbols. On one wall is the ivory crucifix that belonged to Sir Henry Irving and hung above his bed, and some framed David Garrick memorabilia ('*Off* the stage he was a mean sneaking little fellow', wrote a fellow professional, Arthur Murphy, 'but on the stage . . . oh, my great God!'[1]) that belonged to Laurence Olivier and were given by his widow, Joan Plowright, after his memorial service. Quite a hotch-potch of treasures. Around the walls I asked an artist to paint some words of Boethius, in Helen Waddell's translation:

> To see thee is the end and the beginning,
> Thou carriest me and thou dost go before,
> Thou art the journey and the journey's end.

For they say it all.

Boethius was born in Italy, probably in 482, the same year as St Benedict, the founder of the order of monks which served the Abbey monastery until the Reformation. He was a Roman senator, a Christian who became the trusted counsellor of Theodoric, an increasingly intolerant ruler of the Goths. Theodoric became old and wary and suspicious. Boethius came to the defence of one of his fellow consuls who was charged with treason, and was then himself likewise charged, imprisoned at Pavia, tortured and eventually put to death. But not before writing in prison one of the most humane and influential contributions to Western philosophical thought, his *Consolations of Philosophy*, describing in verse and prose how the soul can attain through philosophy to a knowledge of the vision of God. It was widely read in the Middle Ages: translated by King Alfred in the ninth century, by Chaucer in the fourteenth, and by Queen Elizabeth in the sixteenth, traces of its thought can be found in English literature from *Beowulf* through *Hamlet* to Milton's *Lycidas*. It contains a fine passage in praise of human friendship, which Boethius calls 'the most precious treasure in the world'; and in his dungeon, facing his own passion and death, he steadies himself by contemplating the beauty of the natural world seen through the prison bars:

> Look to the highest of the heights of heaven,
> See where the stars still keep their ancient peace.

This was the man whose words about God being both 'the journey and the journey's end' I chose to have painted on the white walls of the Abbot's Pew, for they express the central truth about whose we are and what our end is to be.

The other room that links both the Abbey and what was our home is the remarkable room built in the late fourteenth century in the time of Abbot Litlyngton as the Abbot's State room, the Jerusalem Chamber. It is still formally part of the Deanery. Henry IV, taken ill while praying in the Shrine on the eve of leaving for the Holy Land, was placed on a pallet and rushed to the Abbot's House where they laid him before the fire in what had always been called the Jerusalem Chamber. In the *Second Part of King Henry IV* Shakespeare sets the scene of his death here. Prince Hal is summoned to his bedside. Thinking the king has died, they have covered his face with a linen cloth and the prince removes the crown. His father recovers consciousness and Prince Hal is summoned back and (more gently in a contemporary chronicler's account than in Shakespeare's) rebuked. What Shakespeare does not record is that the future Henry V spent the whole night at the Abbey in prayer, largely (according to tradition) in the company of the resident anchorite, a senior monk who had a cell of his own, and whose cell lay close to St Benedict's Chapel. It was the Abbey anchorite whom Richard II had consulted before going to face Wat Tyler, and another anchorite who now helped Hal bridge the gap between the Boar's Head tavern and the throne. Strangely, I had played the role of Hal and the scene of the king's death in a school production of the play, the beginning of a lifelong passion for the theatre.

It therefore delighted me that there was so strong a link between the Abbey and the stage. Irving's crucifix, a letter and a lock of hair of David Garrick that had belonged to Olivier (all three buried in Poets' Corner near the statue of Shakespeare), and the latter's powerful treatment of Henry's death in the Jerusalem Chamber, were a daily reminder of the alliance of drama and religion. The earliest Greek drama had recognised both its moral and psychological role. Great men who showed a self-confident contempt for a divine moral order, and their proper place within it, demonstrated the flaw of *hubris*. They had to be punished. That aroused in the audience a healthy pity and terror, what Aristotle in his *Poetics* describes as that purging of strong emotion in the process known as *catharsis*. But comedy as well as tragedy had a cathartic role; the Greek comedians, by their use of exaggeration, showing the absurdity of us all, an absurdity recognised and purged by the catharsis of laughter. Molière, Ibsen, Chekhov and Wilde stand in this same tradition and serve the same purpose; and Shakespeare has a unique ability to juggle 'the mystery of things' with the often absurdity of everyday life: not just Hamlet, Prospero and Cleopatra but Aguecheek, Dogberry and Bottom. In Peter Brook's words:

[Shakespeare's] aim ... is holy, metaphysical, yet he never makes the mistake of staying too long on the highest plane. He knew how hard it is for us to keep company with the absolute – so he continually bumps us down to earth.[2]

Not that the drama and the church have always been easy bedfellows. At the end of the fourth century, three years before St Augustine (a great lover of the theatre in his youth but now turned condemnatory) wrote his *Confessions*, actors were excommunicated. The Normans introduced sacred drama into England. Initially closely linked to the rituals in the church, with dramatic embellishments known as tropes inserted into the mass at Christmas, Good Friday and Easter, by the early Middle Ages it moved into the churchyard, then into the streets of the town. In 1311 the feast of Corpus Christi was proclaimed, and it became the major festival for processions and various kinds of civic pageantry. Within the next hundred years the trade guilds began to perform their mystery plays – the Chester, York and Wakefield cycles – often the biblical stories most appropriate to their craft or 'mystery' (the Last Supper acted by the Guild of Bakers, the Passion and Crucifixion by the Arrow-makers, the Coopers and the Ironmongers, the Descent into Hell – inevitably – by the Cooks).

At the Reformation the feast of Corpus Christi was abolished, and the mystery cycles began to die out, to be succeeded by the much duller and more respectable non-biblical morality plays, performed by professional players who travelled from town to town. Only when the London theatres were built in Elizabethan times – the Rose, the Swan and the Globe – was the scene set for the flowering of the true magicians: Christopher Marlowe, Shakespeare and Ben Jonson. The latter possessed an attractive quirkiness: from Westminster School he became a bricklayer, a soldier, an actor; he killed a man in a duel, converted to Catholicism while awaiting trial, and remained in the faith until 1610, when it is said – to celebrate his reconciliation with the Anglican church – he drank the whole of the Communion chalice. In his old age he lived in a house outside the walls of Henry VII's Chapel, the Dean and Chapter sending him £5 when he became paralysed.[3] He is buried in the Abbey nave standing on his feet: being offered a place in Poets' Corner by Dean John Williams, Jonson replied, 'I am too poor for that. No, sir, six feet long by two feet wide is too much for me: two feet by two feet will do for all I want.' 'You shall have it,' said the Dean. And he got it.

The theatre is the place where the human condition may best be explored with touching power and perception, a space which demands the total involvement of both actors and audience, where at its best actors and audience forget themselves and transcend the limitations of their surroundings. Perhaps no theatre setting has been more remarkable than that in the hideous Warsaw Ghetto in the winter of 1942. Of its opening Dr Lazar Epstein wrote:

People laughed and cried. They cast off the depression that had been weighing on their spirits. The alienation that had hitherto existed among the Ghetto population seemed to have been thrown off . . . people awoke from a long difficult dream.[4]

When it comes to presenting and taking part in our liturgies and using our holy spaces, there is much we can learn from it. If that experience we crave beyond the humdrum is to be achieved in the theatre, if we are to emerge at the end having not only been taken out of ourselves but enabled to share a certain vision, then there must not only be huge professional care and concentration by the actors, but also a proper giving of attention by the audience, a mutual give-and-take, which when it happens closes the circle, as it were, and works the magic. In his book *The Empty Space* Peter Brook describes what he calls *holy* theatre, or the theatre of 'the invisible made visible'. He draws the analogy of what happens at a concert, when a group of ordinary people are somehow transformed, almost possessed, as one man waves a stick and the rest scrape their fiddles, and blow their horns, flutes and oboes, by this magical thing called music. Most theatre-goers will affirm that they have had an experience of holy theatre, a performance, say, of *Oedipus* or *Lear* or *Uncle Vanya*, done with passion and with love, that transcends their daily experience, fires the spirit and enables them to glimpse the face of the invisible. But we only sense that indefinable something more that can take your breath away if wearisome effort and professional skill go into the presentation of the play or the music.

Or the liturgy. Nothing matters more in the ordering of our churches than the quality of our worship and the care and imagination we bring to arranging the space we have to fill. Simple, unfussy ceremonial matters. Movement and colour matter. Voice production, pace and the use of silence matter. So does the length of services. I have frequently felt the force of Isaiah's words at the end of over-long services: 'Is it a small thing for you to weary men, but will ye weary my God also?'[5] Worship that is ill-prepared and ill-conducted and is therefore what Brook calls 'deadly theatre', or those who have lost any sense of wonder or mystery in celebrating the Eucharist and any sense of the numinous in conducting worship, are the commonest factor in emptying churches. What is this space for? It is where we human beings, in all our marvellous diversity, may sometimes engage with the transcendent; for the space we have inherited is not just any old space, but a holy space, the place where past generations have met in search of that encounter between the seen and the unseen.

So these links with drama in the Abbot's Pew and the Jerusalem Chamber served to remind me of lessons to be learned from the theatre. And these two places, part of my work-place and my home, reminded me too that (however closely meshed with the Abbey it might be) I also had a private life. Basically, I was me. Clergy, and certain other professional people, can easily be entirely taken over by their occupational roles. I have already written of this in Chapter 3. Of how, like actors, we play our parts: sometimes (like bad actors) inproperly and in a negative sense, by distancing ourselves from people with a kind of protective authority; but often quite properly, and without in any sense losing our humanity, by performing certain acts – leading worship, conducting a wedding or a funeral, hearing a confession or counselling – when what people require of us is a skilled and expert professionalism. But we must recognise when we need to be 'in role' and when we don't. I needed over the years to learn to stand on both feet: to set alongside the daily activities deriving from my job – the worship, the preaching, the administration, the counselling of individuals, the planning, the chairing of meetings – those other, more personally chosen activities that claimed me.

Paradoxically, one of my best of days, when I was both totally playing a role and yet totally 'out of role', was in the theatre. One day in 1995 a friend told me that Peter Hall, for his RSC production of *Julius Caesar* at Stratford, had insisted on a large crowd of extras and that they were using amateurs for the first time in years. He was one of them. Knowing that I had acted in Peter Hall's first productions when we were fellow-undergraduates at Cambridge, he asked if I would like to be a 'fill-in' extra at a Saturday matinée. So one Saturday in December I travelled to Stratford and on the stage where, as an entranced schoolboy, I had watched Godfrey Tearle and Diana Wynyard as Othello and Desdemona, and Paul Scofield and Claire Bloom as Hamlet and Ophelia, I played a Roman senator, a citizen and a soldier. It was a particularly blood-filled production, and after the murder of Caesar in the Senate House, we all escaped into the narrow trench that runs under the front of the Stratford stage. As the conspirators filed past us in that confined space, their daggers dripping blood, I thought that in the Abbey choral evensong would just be starting and wished my colleagues could see me.

But my two other chosen private concerns were a bit more sober. They had to do with what the Palm Sunday collect describes as God's **'tender love towards mankind'**, and in two particular areas. The first concerned human rights for those seeking asylum in Britain; the second, the care of the dying. The Bible is explicit about how we should treat strangers and refugees. The Hebrew people, having suffered so much during their long exile in Egypt, felt a moral obligation to be merciful to exiles:

Do not oppress the alien, for you know how it feels to be an alien; you yourselves were aliens in Egypt.[6]

Put that beside Jesus' familiar words:

When I was hungry, you gave me food; when thirsty, you gave me drink; when I was a stranger, you took me into your home; . . . anything you did for one of my brothers here, however insignificant, you did for me.[7]

and there is no escaping the obligation of hospitality.

The facts are bleak. Whereas in the past Britain had a fine record of welcoming those fleeing from persecution – the Huguenots, the Nazi-persecuted Jews, the Ugandan Asians, the 'boat-people' from Vietnam – in the 1980s and 1990s there have been increasingly restrictive measures against those from nations in Africa, the Indian sub-continent and the Middle East who escape from vicious tyrannies and seek asylum here. In 1987 four thousand refugees arrived in Britain seeking asylum. If all had been accepted they would have formed 0.02 per cent of the population. Many come with substantial work and educational qualifications, though a good number, especially victims of torture, are in some physical and psychological distress. A refugee, in terms of the UN Convention, is one who 'has a well-grounded fear of persecution' in his or her own country. The UN Declaration of Human Rights gives everyone the right 'to seek and enjoy in other countries asylum from persecution'. It does not give a person the right to find asylum. The only right an asylum-seeker has is the right not to be removed from Britain while his or her case is being considered.

Numbers have increased since 1987, and no one pretends such decisions are anything but complex. Many leave their countries for economic reasons. Many make false claims. Governments are anxious when those awaiting arbitration or the result of an appeal (and for years the backlog of claimants has been daunting) are receiving social security benefits, and they must protect their citizens at times of severe unemployment. Yet for the past two decades the more restrictive measures, a breakdown in the arbitration and appeal system, the failure to devise a method of distinguishing between valid and invalid claimants, and the increasing use of detention in prison, have produced a situation which is often both inhumane and a shameful denial of natural justice.

In 1987, if a man or woman was refused asylum, they were often returned to their country of origin before an appeal was heard. Many came from countries where there was severe repression, large-scale abuse of human rights, perhaps civil war. A group of us, individuals united simply by their humanitarian concern and (except for me) by their long experience of working for different refugee bodies, came together to form Charter 87, a charter for refugees. I agreed to chair the launch in the Jerusalem Chamber, which looks out onto Broad Sanctuary, so named because for centuries the Abbey was a safe place of sanctuary, a privilege belonging to the monastery from the earliest times, a right much abused as thieves, murderers and vagabonds took refuge from the law, and finally abolished under James I. Yet there is a sense in which our churches should still be places of sanctuary for the oppressed and the damaged. Moreover the Abbey has stood for nearly a thousand years at the heart of a nation which has a proud record of championing the values originally drawn up in Magna Carta.

20 October 1987

Sixty people gather in the Jerusalem Chamber for the launch of the new Charter for Refugees. Among them are refugees from South Africa, Chile, Turkey, Zaire and the Argentine. Many have known persecution and torture and already found sanctuary in Britain: others still await the outcome of their application for asylum. The Charter has been signed by the Archbishops of Canterbury and York, Cardinal Hume and the Chief Rabbi, and several Law Lords. An address is given by Dame Cicely Saunders, married to a man who came to Britain as a Polish refugee. But the unforgettable memory will be that of Dame Peggy Ashcroft, this cause always close to her heart, who reads two poignant psalms: Psalm 137, a psalm of longing for their homeland by people in exile:

> By the waters of Babylon we sat down and wept:
> when we remembered thee, O Sion;

and Psalm 126, a psalm of thanksgiving on their return home:

> When the Lord turned again the captivity of Sion:
> then were we like unto them that dream.
> Then was our mouth filled with laughter:
> and our tongue with joy.

In the next decade an increasingly jaded government did little to improve matters. Each Asylum Bill was more draconian than the last. The steering group of Charter 87 continued to meet regularly in the Deanery. We harassed the Home Office, edited a newsletter, took up individual cases of excessive detention and suicides in detention.[8] The worst time was when, in 1996, the government withdrew all benefits from those asylum-seekers who were awaiting the hearing of an appeal, and from any who did not claim asylum the moment their feet touched British soil, even though some of them may have been tortured and terrorised and helped to escape, arriving traumatised and knowing no English. Three Court of Appeal Judges ruled unanimously that asylum seekers have a right to food and shelter, but it made no difference.

10 August 1996

Alison and I visit a feeding and advice Day Centre for asylum seekers deprived of all benefits in a Methodist church in Vauxhall. We take a cheque from the Abbey's One People Fund for £5000. The Centre opens for four hours daily. It is run by volunteers and sponsored by the local churches, plus a grant from the London Boroughs. There is a sense of baffled hopelessness. Many have walked from the farthest outskirts of London in order to have a hot meal, some legal advice and a bit of company. I talk to a man who has been tortured in Iran; a woman whose family were killed and who was raped by soldiers in Zaire; another tells me, through his tears, that he has just heard that his brother has been murdered in Algeria. All are homeless and penniless.

There has been much talk this year of morality. Morality is at heart about giving proper value to every human being, and any Christian critique of society must begin by judging how it treats the poor, the disadvantaged and the stranger in its midst.

In October 1997 we decided that Charter 87 should have a final meeting, again in the Jerusalem Chamber. In ten years a number of other effective bodies have sprung up to defend the rights of refugees. The same two psalms are read by a rabbi, and poems by former refugees. The new Home Office Minister for Refugees is present. Before the election the present Home Secretary promised that Labour 'would make a fresh start on immigration and asylum policy... operating policies which honour Britain's obligation under international law'. To date not a great deal has changed, and, as I write, Sir David Ramsbotham, the Chief Inspector of Prisons, has said that the existing policy for dealing with asylum-seekers and the Immigration Service itself is 'a complete and utter shambles' and has called for major changes. They cannot come too soon.

Having got that off my chest, I went to London yesterday to ride on a hoist to the top of the Albert Memorial, currently being massively restored, and to admire that astonishing epitome of Victorian Gothic art, created for 'a grateful nation' to honour Prince Albert – himself 18 foot from head to toe and smothered in gold leaf – by Sir Giles Gilbert Scott, who earlier, as the Abbey's Surveyor, had plastered an excessive amount of gold leaf on the opulent reredos he designed to stand behind the Abbey's high altar, successfully opposed a proposal to demolish St Margaret's Church to improve the view of the Abbey, and is buried in the nave. But my real purpose was to see the perfect film for Passiontide: the Russian director Alexandr Sokurov's *Mother and Son*. It is a slow, tender and endlessly touching account of a mother dying in poverty and being watched over by her son. It is the mirror image of Good Friday. The tenderness of Jesus as he **'suffers death upon the cross'** relates to the figures of Mary and John. He is the one Mary has carried in her womb; the one to whom she has taught his first stumbling words; taught (wonderfully, mysteriously) the one who is in the world to reveal the Father's love and the Father's will, what it means to love and be loved, and what it means to do the Father's will. Taught him how to move from the proper dependence of the child to the correct independence of the man. Taught him all she could – and then let him go. And after that long-drawn-out death on Golgotha, artists have chosen that moment when the body is taken down from the cross to create their *pietàs*, with Jesus once more held and cradled in his mother's arms. In Sokurov's film it is the son who undergoes the Passion, who watches beside his mother, cradling her in his arms, and then, in a long *pietà*-like sequence, lifts her at her request and takes her in his arms for a last lingering walk in the lush countryside around their home.

It is a film that is reticent (an unfashionable attribute) almost to the point of silence. Like God himself. Nothing is more important to our understanding of the Christ-like God than what Holy Week finally shows: that a combination of freedom and love implies not an absent God (though it often feels like that) but a reticent one. I love Kierkegaard's words:

God . . . picks his steps more carefully than if angels guided them, not to prevent his foot from stumbling against a stone, but lest he trample human beings in the dust, in that they are offended in him. He is the God, and yet his eye rests upon mankind with deep concern, for the tender shoots of an individual life may be crushed as easily as a blade of grass.[9]

What Jesus shows in these last days is that God's way is not to coerce us by force or by some undeniable evidence of his power. That would be to cripple our freedom. But to allow us to do with him what we will – ignore him, deny him, crucify him – and to wait and to endure with the authority of an unchanging love. Nowhere is Jesus more powerful than in his passive suffering on the cross. Nowhere does he show more clearly the truth of the reticent, vulnerable God whose hands are tied by his 'tender love'. In the Palm Sunday collect we ask that 'we may follow the example of (Christ's) patience and humility'. And not least when we too come to die.

Which brings me to my other private activity. When the story of our century is told, I guess one of the most significant advances will be seen to have been in the field of palliative care, the relief of pain and the creation of hospices. In earlier centuries death was a public event – even on occasion, like crucifixion, a public entertainment – and dying was often messy, drawn-out and painful. We, understandably but foolishly, have tried to keep death out of sight. Medical advances guarantee that we shall live both longer and better, but there is a cost: more of us will suffer some terminal or degenerative illness. And because we fear being in pain, or helpless, or alone, increasingly there is talk of euthanasia and living wills. Yet, thanks to the work of pioneers like Dame Cicely Saunders, the hospice movement has wonderfully transformed the process of dying, both by the part it has played in the development of pain control (so that only a tiny percentage of cancer patients need now suffer pain in any serious way), and in ensuring that specialist hospice units are being developed worldwide. The best of them honour the original meaning of the word 'hospital', a place of hospitality which has the feeling of home.

For the past ten years I have served on the Council of St Christopher's Hospice in south London, which Dame Cicely Saunders still chairs. Founded in 1967, it cares for almost half the cancer patients in its huge catchment area, some two thousand people annually, as well as being a centre for research and education, giving advice to many other professionals. Most of us would like to die at home, and nearly half of those treated are in what is called 'home care', with regular nursing visits; some come into St Christopher's to have their medication for pain control established and then return home; others are nursed during their final days or weeks in the Hospice. A hospice's task is to assess what each patient (and his or her immediate family) needs and wants, and then deliver it. Each person's time of dying, like their life or their illness, is unique to them, a time when for many there will be a search for meaning and a need to be valued and affirmed as, perhaps, many have never been before. Each one has a story and a culture, beliefs and anxieties, and needs to be listened to and respected for the singular person he or she is, an embodied spirit, an ensouled body. The hospital ethic is too often, 'How can we do everything possible to prevent you dying?'; the hospice ethic,

'You are dying. How can we do everything possible to enable you to live to the full in the time that is left to you?' In the Children's Hospice in Belarus, caring for so many of the huge number of children still suffering and dying as a result of the nuclear explosion at Chernobyl in 1986, there is this prayer:

When my life is finally measured in
Months, weeks, days, hours . . .
I want to live free of pain,
Free of indignity, free of loneliness.
Give me shelter;
Give me your hand;
Give me your understanding;
Give me your love;
Then let me go peacefully,
And help my family understand.

The dying of Jesus begins and ends with the same word, *Father*. 'Father, forgive them'; 'Father, into your hands I entrust my spirit.' Father: 'Abba'. It is one of the few Aramaic words in the New Testament and a word Jesus made peculiarly his own. It expresses a wonderful intimacy with God, this word, with its mixture of reverence and affection, the word with which a Jewish child addressed a parent. It seems to have been Jesus' deep conviction that everything we experience is undergirded by love. He never claimed that God would protect us from the violence of life. Those who witness to what is true and good and just and honest may well be called upon to suffer, even to die, as Jesus did. But what he did say was that 'not a sparrow falls to the ground without your Father [knowing]'. He saw every natural event as within the purpose and care of God, and for him death is included in God's fatherliness. Like every other human experience it is an occasion for trust.

So it is the word 'Abba' that sets the seal on Jesus' life, as it is the 'Our Father' that is the basic Christian prayer at all times and in all places; and for the Christian all our questioning of life should be within the context of God's loving care. Not a belief that we shall be protected when others are not. I may lose my child from leukaemia; I may be struck down by sickness; and it is certain that I and those I love most dearly will die one day, but we can now say with far greater reason than Job had: 'Though he slay me yet will I trust him', for 'underneath are the everlasting arms'.

'Father, into your hands I entrust my spirit.' The words from Psalm 31, that verse from the Jewish prayer book that was to be said last thing at night before falling asleep, were no doubt taught him by his mother. They convey the simplest, most childlike form of trust. Jesus had often spoken of the only true way to live: the way of letting go of all that claims us, of dying daily in small ways. For when we come to die finally we cannot hold on to anything: not our loved ones or friends, not our position or possessions, not even our freedom to do good or ill. All has to go. In this way our physical death becomes a kind of final parable of how to attempt to live the whole of life, letting go, letting God take over, learning to enter the kingdom with open hands like a child receiving gifts.

On that first Good Friday Pilate had an inscription written and nailed to the cross. It read: 'Jesus of Nazareth, King of the Jews' in Hebrew, Latin and Greek. The people mocked him, challenging him to come down from the cross. Some, no doubt, challenged him, if he was truly a king, to reign from there. The existence of the Abbey and of every other church in Christendom – and even, maybe, the fact that I am writing this book and that you are reading it – is proof that he does.

Almighty and everlasting God,
who in your tender love towards mankind
  sent your Son our Saviour Jesus Christ
to take upon him our flesh
and to suffer death upon the cross:
grant that we may follow the example
  of his patience and humility,
sensitive to all in need and treating them with tender care;
and help us, when we come to die,
to share his trust in your enduring love,
and also be made partakers of his resurrection;
through Jesus Christ our Lord.

EASTER DAY

The Abbey

On the hope of resurrection; and on being re-membered

Lord of all life and power,
who through the mighty resurrection of your Son
overcame the old order of sin and death
to make all things new in him:
grant that we, being dead to sin
and alive to you in Jesus Christ,
may reign with him in glory;
to whom with you and the Holy Spirit
be praise and honour, glory and might,
now and in all eternity.

26 February 1990

This week Nelson Mandela has been released from his imprisonment on Robben Island. It is the first positive sign that 'the old order of sin and death' that has marred the life of South Africa for generations is being overcome. To celebrate this some hundred people gather in the quire on a cold evening at this darkest time of the year. Bishop Trevor Huddleston reads from Isaiah and *Naught for your Comfort*. Representatives from South Africa – a refugee, a student, a member of the ANC, Dennis Goldberg, imprisoned with Mandela and released after 23 years – light candles and name individual martyrs such as Steve Biko; and then douse them as we stand in silent remembrance. Then Archbishop Runcie relights them from last year's Easter candle, and a trio of black South African women sing in the darkened Abbey a tender African lamentation. A child, the daughter of a detainee, leads us in the Lord's Prayer; then the three women sing the ANC (soon to become the new South African) anthem 'Nkosi sikelel-i Africa', God Bless Africa.

Tonight I remember a passage from the diary of Brother Roger Schutz, Prior of Taizé, visiting South Africa at the height of apartheid:

> I thought we should be meeting a few friends, but a whole crowd had gathered for prayer . . . African priests and pastors of all denominations welcomed me on a platform and handed me a microphone. [I spoke some words to them] but I said to myself that my words were so inadequate. [So instead] I tried to express all that was in my heart with a gesture. 'I would like to ask your forgiveness, not in the name of the whites – I could not do that – but because you are suffering for the Gospel and you go before us into the Kingdom of God. I would like to pass from one to another of you so that each of you can make the sign of the cross on my palm, the sign of Christ's forgiveness.' This gesture was understood immediately. Everyone made it, even the children. It seemed to take an eternity. And then, spontaneously, they burst into songs of resurrection.[1]

20 July 1994

Today two thousand people fill the Abbey for a joyful service to welcome South Africa back into the Commonwealth, which it left in 1961. Until that year, the High Commissioner had a permanent stall in the Abbey and was invited to Evensong annually on South Africa Day – as is every Commonwealth High Commissioner throughout the year – but the wooden inscription was removed and placed in store for what had seemed the unlikely day when the years of apartheid were ended. Today the plaque is back in place.

The Speaker, the Lord Chancellor, the Duchess of Kent and the Queen Mother are present. President Mandela was coming, but is recovering from an eye operation, and his place is taken by Deputy-

President Mbeki. During the first hymn the 50 flags of the Common-wealth nations are carried the full length of the Abbey by their nations' representatives in national dress and placed in stands grouped on either side of the high altar, leaving one stand empty. Janet Suzman reads from Alan Paton's *Cry, the Beloved Country*, and the High Commissioner reads from Colossians ('Put on garments that suit God's chosen and beloved people: compassion, kindness, humility, gentleness, patience'[2]), and as we sing 'Love divine' the flag of the new Republic is carried from the far end of the nave through the choir by some young South African naval officers, and at the chancel steps handed to the Deputy President, who hands it to the Commonwealth Secretary General. He places it in the empty stand, and the congregation erupts into prolonged and spontaneous applause.

In his address Archbishop Desmond Tutu speaks of a transfiguring, resurrection-like experience:

> I entered a polling-booth at the election for the first time in my 62 years, having wondered, in the face of the viciousness of apartheid, whether indeed I was a child of God, and emerged and said: 'Hey, I'm free! My human dignity, so long trampled underfoot, has been restored.' . . . The remarkable courage of a De Klerk and the magnanimity and lack of bitterness of a Nelson Mandela finally brought this beautiful land to her senses, and like the prodigal she is returning home and getting a wonderful welcome . . . And we can only say: 'Wow!'

High on the choir screen the Elite Swingsters from Soweto, their soloist Dolly Rathebe dressed in breath-taking crimson and gold and caught in a shaft of sunlight, play and sing a 'Peace Song for South Africa' and we all sing '*Nkosi sikelel-i Africa*'. Afterwards Desmond Tutu and Trevor Huddleston embrace, and Tutu dances for joy in the Abbey forecourt.

9 July 1996

Nelson Mandela is in London. He comes within hours to the Abbey to lay a wreath on the Tomb of the Unknown Warrior. I am warned he is running late and will not have time to see the Abbey. On the contrary: he wants to see everything, to meet everyone and to give them his undivided attention. At the gate stands a new Abbey marshal, who began work only yesterday. Mandela alights from his car and at once stops, shakes his hand and talks to him. After the wreath-laying and the prayers I take him on a tour. At the quire entrance the choristers sing to him and he insists on shaking hands and speaking with all 22 of them. Near the Shrine he places a hand on my arm and says: 'I never cease to be grateful to the Church: without it I should have had no education and I should not be here.' His effect on those in the Abbey is to mirror in miniature his effect on London in the next three days: wherever he goes there are crowds and people feel reassured. Mandela is no plaster saint: every great man or woman has their Achilles' heel. The future of South Africa, with its struggling economy and fragmented society, remains unpredictable. Yet, as Tutu said, if something as apparently intractable as apartheid can be resolved without a bloody civil war, then nowhere in the world can there be a problem that the world believes to be intractable. And in Mandela people are responding to that rare and costly authority that is shaped by suffering and validated by the most powerful action in the world: an unembittered readiness to forgive.

Which is the definitive lesson of Good Friday and Easter, a dying that brings forth new life. A dying to the clamour of self; a dying to prejudices and past hurts, to remembered injustice and unforgiven words and actions; a dying to my needs and desires for the sake of the greater good of another; the principle is consistent, whether the scale is the family unit or the nation, the persistent love of a parent for a destructive child or this Good Friday's milestone in the obstinate pursuit of peace in Northern Ireland.

When I chose Ophelia's 'Pray, love, remember' for the title of this book it was because these three words seem to me to sum up the essence of the Christian life, and none more so than the word we asked the sculptor to carve larger than all the rest on that new memorial for the innocent victims of our time: the word *remember*. Why do we need to remember? Because the opposite to remember is to forget, and what is forgotten can never be healed or forgiven. To remember past hurts is the only possible way of allowing our memories to be healed and so to help prevent a greater evil. Such healing is complex, for only those who have been sinned against have the right to forgive. Yet, as George Santayana said: 'He who forgets the past is doomed to repeat it.' It is certainly true of the pastoral counselling that is so central to every priest's ministry that the suffering we most often encounter has to do with wounded, wounding memories that need healing. And if we are to be 'living reminders', then we have no more important task than offering people a space in which such wounding memories may be recalled and brought back into the light without fear or condemnation. Such remembering is usually painful, but only that which is costly is life-giving.

20 August 1995

It is the 50th anniversary of VJ Day, the end of the Second World War, and tonight the Sunday evening service takes the form of a joint British and Japanese service of remembrance. A more formal service is being held at St Paul's Cathedral by the Burma Star Association. Those who spent long years in the unspeakable cruelty and deprivation of Japanese prisoner-of-war camps were resolved that their service should contain no mention of forgiveness or reconciliation, and I can understand that. Only those who have been deeply damaged have the right to speak of forgiveness. Yet there were other survivors who saw things differently, those who for the past decade have been working with contacts in Japan to bring about the healing of memories, costly as that may be. I was approached by the Burma Campaign Fellowship Group, who asked if we would hold a service to be attended by many Japanese who fought in the war as well as the British ex-prisoners. It is an unusually heartfelt service in which we all ask for forgiveness and renew our commitment to peacemaking. The Abbey's Japanese chaplain, a former wartime naval pilot, and Masao Hirakubo, who served in the Japanese Army at Kohima, read the prayers. We end with the whole congregation processing to the Grave of the Unknown Warrior, where British and Japanese children place strings of 6000 multi-coloured paper cranes on the grave, as is the custom on war graves in Japan. At the door many of the veterans are in tears, and it has clearly proved to be one of those acts of worship which meets the needs of those who have suffered in a deeply traumatic way at the hands of their fellows, and helps them face creatively events in the long past, however terrible they may have been. I do not know any other building that can speak as powerfully to people of all nations of inhumanity and the costliness of war.

'Remember'. Nothing is more mysterious than the human brain, nothing harder to explain than this thing we call memory, nerve cells that are soft as butter with little threads of nerve fibre running down between them, which hold the memories of a lifetime. When I look back at my life, all the people I have known and loved, and all the places to which I have ever been, are somehow still part of me. They all live deep inside me whether I like it or not. Until something, a word, a scent or a taste, or a piece of music, can bring a scene or a person flooding back as vividly as if it was yesterday. 'Each of us remembers and forgets,' writes Philip Roth, 'in a pattern whose labyrinthine wanderings are an identification mark no less distinctive than a fingerprint.'[3] Indeed, what chiefly distinguishes us from one another is not only our characters but our memories. For consider what it means for the mystery that is me, and in this other mystery we call 'time', to say 'I remember'. It means that my life is both linear and instant. Here, inside my head, I am all I have ever been: the six-year-old me beginning to pine for my lost father; the eighteen-year-old me at school playing Hamlet and arrogantly thinking I was the new Gielgud; the thirty-something-year-old me falling deeply in love for the first time; the fifty-year-old me over-stressed in a large parish; the sixty-eight-year-old me still (just about) in the first fine careless rapture of retirement and during these past weeks reliving the memories of that Abbey decade. All co-exist inside the mystery I call 'me'. The past and the present are one in the moment that is now, and it is because we are all we have ever been that we can recover, and, as it were, re-member, reassemble, those we have loved and lost, putting them together again, bringing them out of the past and into the present.

Those (like Proust, with his 'madeleine-dipped-in-tea' experience) who have written of the power of such involuntary memories have seen them as a way of overcoming the gap between past and present, for the memories thus recalled seem not only to exist outside time, but our apparently fragmentary selves can be given a unity by this kind of reliving of our past in the present. We discover that we are a consistent whole, that we can find our true selves, the self that is continuous throughout our lives. We learn that we change in many ways: we are scarred by grief; hopefully we grow in those cardinal qualities of trust and love; yet, even in old age, we still feel we are the same as we always were. It is as if there has been a pattern which we certainly could not predict before the plot of our lives unfolded, but which now in retrospect is seen to make sense. And such recollection gives pleasure because it is a kind of reconstruction of our lives. By using both memory and imagination, we can *re-member* our lives, put them together again, discover the threads that bind them together and find they form a whole.

A great Jewish rabbi, Abraham Joshua Heschel, said: 'Much of what the Bible demands can be comprised in one word: Remember.'[4] The Bible's view is first and foremost that when we remember something from the past we make it present again, make it once more potent in our lives for good or ill. So, for example, in the Old Testament it is essential for the people of Israel that God's love in the past should not be forgotten, that even when things are at their darkest they are to find their hope and strength in a remembered love which is to sustain them. A love which memory, with its power of transcending time, has the power to bring out of the past into the present. So the annual Passover meal is a thankful remembrance of God's mighty act of deliverance, when Israel was brought out of Egypt and formed into the people of God.

A thankful remembrance. On the night in which he was betrayed, on the eve of a new and even greater deliverance, Jesus takes bread and wine and says: 'Do this in remembrance of me' (in Greek, 'for my "anamnesis" '). The German New Testament scholar Joachim Jeremias says that 'do this in my remembrance' means that, when the community comes together for the breaking of bread, God is being sought to 'remember his Messiah', and to remember his Messiah by bringing about his Kingdom, so that the Eucharist becomes a kind of dramatisation of the prayer 'thy Kingdom come'. But that does not exhaust its meaning. For when the first Christians came together to celebrate the weekly Easter, the 'anamnesis' of the crucified and risen Lord, they believed he would be present in all his living reality in their midst. For them every Eucharist bound together both past and future: the lakeside meals, the Maundy scene of foot-washing, Golgotha and the Easter appearances, as well as the anticipation of what shall be: the whole Gospel is re-membered, re-*present*-ed, put together and made present again, in the 'now' of faith in all its saving power. For there is a sense in which time is transcended, a sense in which faith makes contemporary both the past and the future. Aquinas speaks of the Eucharist as an experience of heaven, and paradoxically, when we take part in the Eucharist we are in truth also remembering the future, remembering that which will be because its essential content has been given us in what has already been. The Orkney writer who died last year, George Mackay Brown, wrote at the end of his autobiography:

The simplest Mass is the most beautiful event imaginable. The scriptural Passion which was its matrix is beyond the imaginative reach of Dante, Shakespeare or Tolstoy.[5]

Time is that necessary invention by which we make sense of our lives, and in the Eucharist we can be said to transcend the sequence of what we may call 'clock-time'. If we are citizens of two realms, with a system of references between them, there is still an unbridgeable gap between them, for they are 'as far and as close to each other as time and calendar, as violin and melody, as life and what lies beyond the last breath'.[6] We are both in clock-time and in what we might call 'significant time': the Proustian 'madeleine-dipped-in-tea' moment, or the moment when we fell in love, or those rare but undeniably transcendent moments when we are caught up out of ourselves. William Blake was able to 'see Infinity in the palm of your hand,/ And eternity in an hour.'[7] T. S. Eliot speaks of the Incarnation as 'the point of intersection of the timeless/ with time'[8] and of Little Gidding as a place 'where prayer has been valid',[9] and it is valid, he says, because 'history is a pattern/ Of timeless moments'.[10] It was Kierkegaard who said that Jesus was able to live without anxiety 'because he had eternity with him in the day that is called today';[11] Jesus, who reveals in time what is eternally true, and in whom we have a relationship with God which transcends time and which that final moment of clock-time we call death has no power to destroy. That linked event, Good-Friday-and-Easter, cross-and-resurrection, is nothing less than the key that unlocks the secret of God's creative power and ultimate purpose for us, as powerful an act as that with which, over unimaginable millennia, God called the universe into being. Baptism has always been seen as the frontier between two worlds: the shift from the old creation and the values of the world to the new creation and the values of that different state of being that we call the Kingdom. In the light of Easter we stand, as it were, with one foot in time and one foot in eternity, for it is in Christ that we catch a glimpse of what eternity is all about, what God is all about, and what we ourselves are ultimately all about too. 'People who dwell in God', wrote Meister Eckhart, 'dwell in the eternal Now'.[12] And our prayer in this moment that is Now is that we may be re-membered.

Re-membered in every sense. For to remember is not only the opposite of 'to forget'; it is also the opposite of 'to dis-member'. To dismember a body is to take it apart, limb by limb, like a man being strung up on a cross until his heart ceases to beat. To re-member someone is to do what all the king's horses and all the king's men couldn't do to Humpty-Dumpty: put him together again. It is to do what only God can do. And both meanings of remember lie at the very heart of the Bible. When the penitent thief says to Jesus: 'Lord, remember me when you come into your Kingdom', I hear the words in the obvious sense of 'Don't forget me'. But I choose to hear him also saying something more profound: 'Lord, re-*member* me, recreate me, make me anew, put me together again, but now in your own likeness and as you have always intended me to be.' For to be re-membered is our destiny. In the end that is our end, our purpose: that is why we are here. That is what every Church on earth exists to do: to bring us into the Kingdom, damaged, dysfunctional people that we are, and re-member us, recreate us as the Body of Christ in the new creation that exists since that first Easter day. We are those who recognise in Christ our true likeness, our proper humanity, the person God desires us to be, and our prayer is: 'Lord, re-member me, refashion me, so that I may share the life of your Kingdom. Remake my life in the shape of your own.'

And his answer? 'If you would truly remember me, if you would bring me out of the past into your present, then do this with bread and wine.' And in our imagination we watch him as he takes bread in his hands and offers it, thanks God for it, breaks it, shares it. Says (by implication):

This is me. This is the pattern of my life. You are now to re-member me, that is to say, to be my body in the world, your lives *offered* to God, your lives lived *thankfully*, your lives *broken* and *shared* in the costly service of others.

And that is why every time we 'do this' we are re-membering him, taking what lies in the past and making it present, making him present. It is a re-embodying of Christ, a re-membering of him in us, our incorporation into his Body, St Paul's constant theme. It was St Chrysostom who said that through receiving the bread and wine we are renewed as 'flesh of Christ's flesh, bone of his bone'; and St Teresa who spoke of Christ now having no body on earth but ours; and St Augustine who wrote of the Eucharist:

As this [bread and wine] when you eat and drink it, is changed into you, so you are changed into the Body of Christ by an obedient and holy life. You are receiving that which [unless you receive unworthily] you have begun to be.[13]

Re-membered as his Body. In the words of Teilhard de Chardin, 'the Incarnation realised, in each individual, through the Eucharist'.[14]

Easter Eve 1996
We begin in the nave in total darkness. Nearly a thousand people have gathered for the dramatic service that will anticipate Easter

Day. Few are regular worshippers, many are from overseas. After the readings, the silences, the prayers, I light the Paschal candle by the west door, and it is carried through the Abbey to its candle-stand by the high altar while the ancient Exultet, the ancient Easter Song of Praise, is sung, and the whole congregation, their individual candles now lit, follow and take their places in the quire and transepts. From the sanctuary hundreds of small flames give a gentle radiance; then, as the Exultet ends and after a New Testament passage is read, Martin Baker (incomparable sub-organist) plays a heart-stopping improvisation which grows louder and more passionate as the lights are progressively turned on in every part. After a prayer and the first hymn of Easter we await the dawning of the new day.

Easter Day 1996

All parts of the Abbey are full to overflowing. Under the Lantern sit the choir and members of the London Chamber Orchestra. The setting is Mozart, the *Coronation Mass*. After the drama of Maundy Thursday, the foot-washing, the descent into darkness, the singing of Allegri's *Miserere*, and the stripping of the altars; after the Good Friday singing of the Passion, the Mystery plays enacted on tableaux in Victoria Street, outside Westminster Cathedral and in the nave of the Abbey, comes this: the climax of the year, a celebration of an experience so unexpected, so radical, so undeniable, that out of it the Church was born, the gospels were written, lives were changed, and all these centuries later we are gathered in this 'serious house on serious earth' to do the Eucharist as it has been done in this space on every Easter Day for over a thousand years. If Christ is not risen, it would not exist and we should not be here. That is the truth to which we witness and that is the mystery. As we begin, the sun is lighting up the golden angels on the great organ. It was C. S. Lewis who said that you cannot look directly at the mystery of Christ's resurrection any more than you can look directly at the sun, yet just as by the sun's light we see the creation exposed in all its beauty, so in the light of Easter we see the reality – and the

130

potential – of the new creation. Everything is changed, and we are not the same as we were before.

Remembering Meister Eckhart's words, that 'if the only prayer you say in your whole life is thank you, that would suffice'; remembering that Jewish writer's claim that at the Day of Judgement God will only ask us one question: 'Did you enjoy my creation?'; and remembering, too, that 'eucharist' means 'thanksgiving', I have sometimes tried to look back on my own journey and make a map of my public and private worlds. In my mind I sort out the threads that have come together and which in retrospect have shaped my life. Starting with childhood, I think about the role that words and language have played, the influence of stories, myths, poems, novels, plays, and especially those particular words and images in the Christian story that have burrowed away at my centre and become part of me. I think of the places that have been important, the buildings, the open spaces, the islands and sea coasts, the shapes and colours and textures of things, that I should like to remember with fondness when I come to die. And last, I try to name those individuals who, by their teaching, their friendship or their love, have made all the difference. To live eucharistically is to desire to set your whole life in the context of thanksgiving; and these are the people, the places and the truths for which and for whom 'it is right at all times and in all places' to be thankful.

Not a day has passed in nearly two millennia when Christians have not remembered the founding events of their faith with the same allegiance as their forebears: this drama of the Eucharist which, like God himself, is both in time and beyond it. For in it we can look back to the past, to this man doing these actions; we can equally look to the future and see people increasingly coming together to break and to share bread (with all that means in our unjust world), people who are open to God and to each other in this new creation we call the Kingdom. But chiefly we may glimpse here the God revealed in Christ who is to be met in each other now or not at all, here or nowhere; re-membered, embodied in us. And by doing this, day in and day out, week in and week out, as the central act of Christian worship, we are not doing something that is inward-looking and exclusive, speaking only to the initiated. On the contrary: we are presenting, in these four acts of taking, thanking, breaking and sharing, the proper pattern and shape for all human life. We are helping to restore, however infinitesimally, the whole of creation to its right relationship with God. Everyone and everything called to become the Body of Christ.

Last September I joined a large party of religious leaders – Christian, Muslim, Jewish – and scientists from all over the world for an ecological symposium on and around the Black Sea. It is many years since Jacques Cousteau uttered those sinister words, 'The oceans are dying', and this is the most polluted sea in the world. There is huge nitrogen pollution, much of it from industrial waste flowing down the Danube, the Dnieper and the Don, which has had a disastrous effect on the algae, the seaweeds and the fish. There has been massive over-fertilisation, the careless use of chemicals, the discharge of untreated sewage. In the 1980s a comb jelly, *Mnemiopsis leidyi*, unexpectedly appeared, perhaps carried in cargo ships from Chesapeake Bay, and soon reached a biomass of a billion tons, consuming plankton and decimating the fish and anchovy harvest. Below 200 metres the sea is now as good as dead, 156 species of fish reduced to 5 in 30 years, its monk seals now extinct.

Hazlitt wrote that 'man is the only species who can laugh or cry because he is the only being who knows the difference between what is and what should be'.[15] The proper stewardship of the creation is a spiritual matter, recognised as such (albeit slowly) by the world's great faiths. The symposium was organised by the Ecumenical Patriarch, and attended by the Orthodox leaders of all seven nations we visited, for the Orthodox make no bones about the fact that despoiling the environment is a sin. Not only is everything interlinked – stars, clouds, rivers, forests, fish, human beings – but past, present and future are all part of a continuum. For Christians the world is sacramental, the place where God's presence is to be found and his grace experienced; it is a gift to be received thankfully and treated lovingly. For the Bible the three great symbols of the end (the purpose) of creation are the garden, the city and the meal: the garden, in which the original creation is set (and the new creation that begins in the Easter garden, with Mary Magdalen so significantly mistaking Jesus for the gardener) and which establishes men and women as stewards of the earth; the city of God, of whose form and beauty we cannot conceive but where all will live in peace; and the meal, the heavenly banquet, of which each Eucharist is a foretaste, and where there is no distinction between rich and poor, male and female, black and white. The implications of those three symbols for our stewardship of the earth do not need spelling out. The American poet and ecologist Wendell Berry links it directly to the Eucharist. He says that we must 'daily break the bread and shed the blood of creation. When we do that knowingly, lovingly and reverently, it is a sacrament. When we do it ignorantly, greedily, clumsily, it is a desecration.'[16] Thus by taking God's gifts of bread and wine, gifts that have been worked on by human hands, and giving thanks for them, we are restoring all matter to what God means it to be, and we are saying that life is good, that it is to be celebrated. Given thanks for.

Dear friends, we are now God's children [writes St John]; what we shall be has not yet been disclosed, but we know that when Christ appears we shall be like him, for we shall see him as he is.[17]

Learning more of God so that we may learn more of whom

we truly are: that is an endless exploration and that, and nothing less than that, is the object of our journey. I do not know what form that recovery of wholeness which is a re-membering may take for that one unknown man who lies in that Abbey grave; nor for the millions who have per-ished in the wars of this and every century, in most cases their human journeys barely begun; nor for those other millions who in their innocence have been devoured by the demons of violence and oppression, but I do know that each one is the child of God. And I know, too, that the way for us who place at the centre of our lives the Passion, the Cross and the Resurrection of Jesus Christ is the way of the generations of Christians who have gone before us: the way of that remembering which is also a re-*membering*. For ulti-mately our churches are feeble shadows of what they should be unless at the heart of them are communities of people who Sunday by Sunday, year in and year out, are *embodying* Christ, recalling into the present and into their daily lives, the life, death and rising of the one who shows us the Father; their persisting desire that, however long it takes, they may be refashioned in his likeness. And so, re-membered when he comes into his Kingdom.

Robert Graves has a poem about the cabbage-white butterfly, which

> Will never now, it is too late,
> Master the art of flying straight,
> Yet has – who knows so well as I? –
> A just sense of how not to fly:
> He lurches here and there by guess
> And God and hope and hopelessness.
> Even the acrobatic swift
> Has not his flying-crooked gift.[18]

I have always had a 'flying-crooked' sort of mind, never having mastered the art of flying straight, and this has turned out to be a cabbage-white sort of book; lurching here and there 'by guess and God and hope and hopelessness'. Partly it has been a love-letter to the Abbey, partly thoughts on some of the Lenten and Easter themes, partly diary, partly reflections on those truths (now that I wear what John Donne called my 'Autumnal face') that have come to matter most: praying, loving and remembering. I began it on Ash Wednesday: I am ending it on the day early in Eastertide when the church commemorates St Anselm. He was born in the year before Edward the Confessor came to the throne; he died in Canterbury as Henry I's Archbishop on the Wednesday in Holy Week in 1109. The collect set for today says it all, and as I type these final words I look from my study window and see in the distance, rising above a clump of chestnut and beech trees bursting into leaf, the tall spire of Salisbury Cathedral, built in the very same years as the present Abbey, where men and women have desired and sought and found God for over eight hundred years; and, being human, will never be content with anything less.

> **Eternal God,**
> **who gave great gifts to your servant Anselm**
> **as a pastor and teacher:**
> **grant that we, like him,**
> **may desire you with our whole heart**
> **and so desiring, we may seek you**
> **and seeking, we may find you;**
> **through Jesus Christ our Lord.**

Notes

All biblical quotations, except where stated otherwise, are from the Revised English Bible (OUP, 1989).

INTRODUCTION

1 Laurence Tanner, *Recollections of a Westminster Reliquary* (John Baker, 1969).
2 Edward Carpenter and David Gentleman, *Westminster Abbey* (Weidenfeld & Nicolson, 1987).

Chapter 1 ASH WEDNESDAY

1 After two years of discussion and planning members of Chapter initiated in March 1998 'Restoring the Calm', a radical experiment on grounds of health and safety to control the numbers of those entering the Abbey by introducing entry charges for the whole building and aiming to make the nave a place for prayer. Only time will show if this proves successful; but something had to be done.
2 Philip Larkin, 'Church Going', *Collected Poems*, (Faber, 1988).
3 Wisdom of Solomon 11:26, 12:1.
4 Edward Robinson, *The Language of Mystery* (SCM Press, 1987) p. 86.
5 Seamus Heaney, *The Government of the Tongue* (Faber, 1988) pp. 23, 106–7.
6 John Bowden, 'Vision' in *Theology*, January 1980.
7 Words often used by Dame Cicely Saunders to express in a phrase the ethos of a good hospice.
8 W. B. Yeats, *Autobiographies* (Macmillan, 1955).
9 Martin Buber, *I and Thou* (T & T Clark, 1937).
10 Gerard Manley Hopkins, 'As Kingfishers Catch Fire', *Collected Poems* (Oxford, 1948).
11 Quoted in Ronald Blythe, *The Age of Illusion* (OUP, 1983), p. 8.

12 ibid.

13 George Steiner, 'Remembering the Future' in *Theology*, Nov/Dec 1990.

14 W. H. Auden, 'Epitaph for the Unknown Soldier', *Collected Poems* (Faber, 1976).

Chapter 2 LENT I

1 e. e. cummings, *Selected Poems* (Faber, 1960).

2 Philip Larkin, 'Church Going', op cit.

3 G. M. Trevelyan, *An Autobiography and Other Essays* (Longman, 1949).

4 R. S. Thomas, 'Folk Tale', *Experimenting with an Amen* (Macmillan, 1986).

5 R. S. Thomas, 'Waiting', *Later Poems* (Macmillan, 1983).

6 Sidney Evans, *Prisoners of Hope* (The Lutterworth Press, 1990) p. 101.

7 ibid.

8 Jeremy Taylor. Source untraced.

9 St Augustine, *Sermons* (de Script NT) 88 v5.

10 William Law, *The Spirit of Prayer* (1728). Quoted in F. C. Happold, *Mysticism* (Penguin, 1963) p. 348.

11 Alan Ecclestone. From a sermon that I cannot now trace.

12 G. B. Caird, *St Luke* (Penguin, 1963) p. 81.

13 Simone Weil, *Concerning the Our Father: Waiting on God* (Routledge & Kegan Paul, 1952) p. 153.

Chapter 3 LENT II

1 Private letter from Mike Wooldridge, now BBC Correspondent in Delhi, quoted with permission.

2 John 14:6.

3 Gerard Hughes, *God, Where Are You?* (Darton, Longman & Todd, 1997) p. 187.

4 John 10:10.

5 Quoted in a lecture by Anita Brookner on the painter Jacques Louis David, and applied by her to the luminous paintings of Howard Hodgkin.

6 Gal. 2:20.

7 George Herbert, 'Aaron', *George Herbert's Verse*, selected by R. S. Thomas (Faber, 1967).

Chapter 4 LENT III

1 G. Rosser, *Medieval Westminster 1200–1540* (OUP, 1989).
2 Quoted in John Field, *Kingdom, Power and Glory* (James & James, 1996) p. 30.
3 Hos. 11: 3–4.
4 Grace Jantzen, 'AIDS, Shame and Suffering' in *Embracing the Chaos: Theological Responses to AIDS* (SPCK, 1990) pp. 28–9.
5 For the record, the actors (and in three cases writers) who read in Personal Choice were: Dame Peggy Ashcroft with Ronald Pickup, Timothy West and Prunella Scales, Paul Scofield and Joy Packer, Joss Ackland, Richard Pasco and Barbara Leigh-Hunt, Alec McCowen, Alan Bennett (twice, once with Merula Guinness), Patricia Routledge, Jane Lapotaire, Sheila Hancock and John Thaw, Peter Barkworth, Dame Judi Dench and Michael Williams, Juliet Stevenson, Sir Alec Guinness, Dame Diana Rigg, Freddie Jones, Joan Plowright with Keith Baxter, Edward Woodward, Michael Denison and Dulcie Gray, Robert Hardy, Tim Pigott-Smith, Sir Ian McKellen, Maureen Lipman, Stephen Fry, Edward Petherbridge and Emily Richard, Sîan Phillips, Griff Rhys Jones, Fiona Shaw, John Julius Norwich, John McCarthy and Jill Morrell, and Christopher Fry.
6 Quoted anonymously in Gerard Hughes, *God, Where Are You?* (Darton, Longman & Todd, 1997) p. 11.
7 Isa. 53:5.
8 William Blake, *Auguries of Innocence.*
9 R. S. Thomas, 'The Word' in *Later Poems 1972–1982* (Macmillan, 1983).
10 Stephen Pattison, *A Critique of Pastoral Care* (SCM, 1993).
11 John 20:15. The link may seem tenuous, but I find it helpful.
12 2 Cor. 4:16–18.
13 Ps. 139:8.

Chapter 5 MID-LENT BREATHER

1 Arthur Penrhyn Stanley, *Memorials of Westminster Abbey*, 5th ed, 1882.
2 Besides John Clare and Oscar Wilde, during my time as Dean, and with the support of Chapter, I also agreed to memorials to Matthew Arnold, Anthony Trollope, Edward Lear, Alexander Pope, Robert Herrick, A. E. Housman, Laurence Olivier and John Betjeman.
3 Brian Patten, *Storm Damage* (Flamingo/HarperCollins, 1995).
4 ibid.
5 Anne Michaels, *Fugitive Pieces* (Bloomsbury, 1997), p. 207.

6 Joseph Conrad, *The Nigger of the Narcissus*, Preface, 1898.

7 ibid.

8 Jay Leyda, *The Years and Hours of Emily Dickinson* (2 vols., 1960), vol. 2, p. 151.

9 Graham Swift, *Ever After* (Picador, 1992), p. 234.

10 R. S. Thomas, 'Emerging' ll.17–18, *Later Poems* (Macmillan, 1983).

11 Ted Hughes, *Winter Pollen* (Faber, 1994), p. 20.

12 Paul Celan, *Collected Prose* (Carcanet, 1986), p. 12.

13 Ted Hughes, op. cit., p. 222.

14 Seamus Heaney, *The Government of the Tongue* (Faber, 1988), p. 107.

15 ibid., pp. 7–8.

16 Ps. 33:6, 9.

Chapter 6   LENT IV

1 John Clare, *Selected Poems and Prose*, ed. Eric Robinson and Geoffrey Summerfield (OUP, 1978) p. 195.

2 Richard Ellmann, *Oscar Wilde* (Hamish Hamilton, 1987) p. 465.

3 Obituary in the *Independent*, 30 April 1998.

4 Ps. 26:8.

5 'There's glory for you!' 'I don't know what you mean by "glory",' Alice said. 'I meant, "there's a nice knock-down argument for you!".' 'But "glory" doesn't mean "a nice knock-down argument",' Alice objected. 'When I use a word,' Humpty-Dumpty said in a rather scornful tone, 'it means just what I choose it to mean – neither more nor less.'

6 2 Cor. 4:6.

7 2 Cor. 3:18.

8 Thomas Merton, essay, 'To each his own darkness' in *Raids on the Unspeakable* (New Directions, New York, 1964).

9 Quoted with the agreement of his family.

10 Horace, *Odes*, iv, 13.

11 Mary Oliver, *New & Selected Poems* (Beacon Press, Boston, 1992), p. 10.

12 Dante, *Paradiso*, XXXIII, 145.

13 Thomas Traherne, *Centuries* (The Clarendon Press, 1960), *The Second Century*, p. 66.

14 David Denby, *Great Books* (Simon & Schuster, New York, 1996), p. 307.

15 A month after I wrote this my mother died, peacefully, aged 96.

16 Frederick Buechner, *The Longing for Home* (HarperSanFrancisco, 1996), p. 28.

17 Anne Michaels, *Fugitive Pieces* (Bloomsbury, 1997), p. 169.

Chapter 7   LENT V

1 William Blake, *Jerusalem* pl. 55, 1, 60
2 Wilfred Owen, 'Futility' in *The Penguin Book of First World War Poetry*, ed. Jon Silkin (Penguin, 1979).

Chapter 8   PALM SUNDAY

1 Simon Trussler, *Cambridge Illustrated History of the Theatre* (CUP, 1994), p. 176.
2 Peter Brook, *The Empty Space*, (Penguin Books, 1972), p. 69.
3 John Field, *Kingdom, Power and Glory*, (James & James, 1996), p. 95.
4 Read, noted and lost.
5 Isa. 7:13 AV.
6 Exod. 23:9.
7 Matt. 25:35, 40.
8 Tribute should be paid to Dr Louise Pirouet and Antonia Hunt, Co-ordinators of Charter 87. Both have been tireless fighters for the rights of refugees, working with stubborn persistence and courage in the face of considerable odds and much official obstinacy.
9 Sören Kierkegaard, *Philosophical Fragments*.

Chapter 9   EASTER DAY

1 Brother Roger of Taizé, *And Your Deserts Shall Flower* (Mowbray, 1983), entry for 24 November 1978.
2 Col. 3:12.
3 Philip Roth, *American Pastoral* (Jonathan Cape, 1997), p. 55.
4 Abraham Joshua Heschel, *Man Is Not Alone* (Farrar, Straus & Giroux, New York, 1951), p. 162.
5 George Mackay Brown, *For the Islands I Sing* (John Murray, 1997), p. 185.
6 Heschel, *Man Is Not Alone* pp. 8–9.
7 William Blake, *Auguries of Innocence* 1.
8 T. S. Eliot, *Four Quartets*. The Dry Salvages V, ll.18–19 (Faber, 1944).
9 *Four Quartets*, Little Gidding I, ll.48–9
10 ibid., V, 11.21–2.
11 Sören Kierkegaard, *Christian Discourses*, trans. Walter Lowrie (OUP, New York, 1961), p. 79.

12 Quoted in Helen Waddell, *Medieval Latin Lyrics* (Gollancz, 1976).
13 St Augustine, *Sermons* 272.
14 Teilhard de Chardin, *Le Milieu Divin* (Collins, 1960), p. 113.
15 William Hazlitt, *Essays* (source untraced).
16 Wendell Berry, essay, 'The Gift of Good Land' in *Standing on Earth* (Golgonooza Press, 1991), p. 98.
17 1 John 3:2.
18 Robert Graves, 'Flying Crooked' in *Poems Selected by Himself* (Penguin, 1957).